25 YEARS *of* FAVORITE BRAND NAME™ *One Dish*

Publications International, Ltd.

Favorite Brand Name Recipes at www.fbnr.com

Pictured on the front cover: Lickety-Split Paella Pronto *(page 243)*.

Pictured on the back cover *(left to right):* Sausage and Broccoli Noodle Casserole *(page 150)* and Farmstand Frittata *(page 54)*.

ISBN-13: 978-1-4127-2491-3
ISBN-10: 1-4127-2491-0

Library of Congress Control Number: 2006903673

Manufactured in China.

8 7 6 5 4 3 2 1

Microwave Cooking: Microwave ovens vary in wattage. Use the cooking times as guidelines and check for doneness before adding more time.

Preparation/Cooking Times: Preparation times are based on the approximate amount of time required to assemble the recipe before cooking, baking, chilling or serving. These times include preparation steps such as measuring, chopping and mixing. The fact that some preparations and cooking can be done simultaneously is taken into account. Preparation of optional ingredients and serving suggestions is not included.

Contents

*W*elcome to the incredible world of one-dish cooking, where complete, delicious, homemade meals are cooked and served all in one dish. Not only can one-dish cooking stretch expensive ingredients, such as meat, but with such easy cleanup, it can save you time in the kitchen too. And with today's busy lifestyles, that's an unbeatable combination!

The three basic types of one-dish meals are casseroles, skillet meals and slow cooker meals.

While some soups, stews and stir-fries can also be considered one-dish meals, not all of them are complete meals. One-dish meals usually include a protein, such as meat or fish, vegetables, and a starch, such as pasta, potatoes, or rice.

Casserole Cookware

Casserole refers both to a specific baking utensil and the food it contains. Casserole cookware comes in a variety of shapes, sizes and materials that fall into two general descriptions. They can be either deep, round containers, or square and rectangular baking dishes. Casserole cookware can be made out of glass, ceramic or metal and may or may not have a cover. When making a casserole, it is important to bake it in the proper size dish so that the ingredients cook evenly in the time specified. Casserole dishes are measured by their volume in quarts. The most common sizes of casseroles are 1, 1½, 2, 2½ and 3 quarts. This container is designed for slow cooking in the oven. Many casseroles are ideal for microwave cooking and some are suitable for use on the stovetop. Check the manufacturer's label to determine if a casserole can be used in these ways.

Determining Dish Size

If you don't know the size of the casserole or baking dish you want to use, and it isn't marked on the bottom of the dish, it can be measured to determine the size.

- **Round and oval casseroles** are measured by volume, not inches, and are always listed by quart capacity. To measure the casserole, fill a measuring cup with water and pour it into the empty casserole. Repeat until the casserole is filled with water, keeping track of the amount of water added. The amount of water is equivalent to the size of the dish.

- **Square and rectangular baking dishes** are usually measured in inches. If the dimensions are not marked on the bottom of a square or rectangular baking dish, use a ruler to measure on top from the inside of one edge to the inside of the opposite edge.

Casserole Dish Substitutions

If you don't have the recommended size of casserole, substitute any ovenproof baking dish in a size that is as large or slightly larger than the recommended one. (A larger dish may require a shorter baking time, so check it sooner than recommended in the recipe.)

If you don't have a:	Use a:
1-quart casserole	8×6-inch baking dish
1½-quart casserole	8×8-inch baking dish
2-quart casserole	8×8-inch or 11×7-inch baking dish
2½-quart casserole	9×9-inch baking dish
3- to 4-quart casserole	13×9-inch baking dish or Dutch oven
5-quart casserole	large Dutch oven or roasting pan

Choosing a Casserole Dish

Whether you're planning to purchase a new casserole dish or just deciding which of your current ones will work for a particular recipe, it helps to know the pros and cons of the many different casserole materials.

Casserole Dishes	Advantages	Disadvantages
enameled cast iron	retains heat well, durable, suitable for range-top use	heavy, usually costly, can chip
stainless steel	durable, inexpensive, suitable for range-top use	poor heat conductor unless bottom is lined with copper or aluminum
ovenproof porcelain or ceramic	inexpensive, retains heat fairly well	cannot be used on range-top, may crack or chip
ovenproof glass	inexpensive, retains heat fairly well	cannot be used on range-top
cast iron	excellent long-term heat retention, very inexpensive, suitable for range-top use	reacts with acidic ingredients, very heavy
aluminum	heats quickly and also cools down quickly, very inexpensive, lightweight	reacts with acidic ingredients, stains easily and can warp, not dishwasher safe
hard-anodized aluminum	retains heat well, suitable for range-top use	expensive, not dishwasher safe

Skillet Meals

Skillet meals are generally easy and quick to prepare, either by simmering all of the ingredients together in the skillet, or by the stir-fry method of cooking. Stir-frying—a rapid cooking method invented by the Chinese—is the brisk cooking of small pieces of ingredients in hot oil over intense heat for a short time. The ingredients are kept in constant motion by stirring or tossing vigorously.

For skillet meals, the most important cooking tool needed is, obviously, your trusty skillet. A skillet, also known as a frying pan, is a round, shallow pan with a straight or slightly sloping side. It is most often used for frying and sautéing. When purchasing a skillet, choose a heavy pan that conducts heat evenly, has a tight fitting cover and a sturdy handle. Skillets range in size from 6 to 14 inches in diameter. A second, short handle opposite the long handle is a great option on larger skillets as it makes them much easier to lift. Most skillet meals for four require a 12-inch skillet.

Stir-fries can be cooked in a skillet or a wok. A wok has a rounded shape with a long sloping side which provides an extended cooking surface; it can be heated to very high temperatures with little fuel. Traditionally a wok was made from thin tempered iron and had a rounded bottom for fast, even conduction of heat. In addition to iron, woks are now made of aluminum, stainless steel and carbon steel. Woks with flat bottoms are made for use on smooth-top cooking surfaces. There are electric woks with nonstick finishes and automatic thermostatic controls. The customary side handles made of metal are sometimes replaced with a single long handle made of material that stays cool. Woks range in size from 12 to 24 inches in diameter. The 14-inch wok is a good choice because it can handle most cooking techniques without interfering with other burners on the range.

Simple Steps for Successful Skillets and Stir-Fries

1. Choose the proper size pan. The size of the skillet or wok that you use is very important in determining how well your food will cook. You can successfully stir-fry a little food in a large skillet or wok, but a lot of food in a small skillet will yield disappointing results.

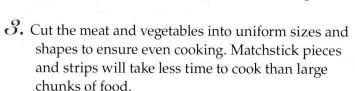

2. Prepare all the ingredients in advance, including cleaning, cutting, measuring and combining.

3. Cut the meat and vegetables into uniform sizes and shapes to ensure even cooking. Matchstick pieces and strips will take less time to cook than large chunks of food.

4. Heavy-duty resealable plastic food storage bags are perfect for marinating ingredients. Any foods marinated for longer than 20 minutes should be marinated in the refrigerator.

5. The best oil to use for stir-frying is peanut oil, corn oil or soybean oil. Olive oil, sesame oil and butter should not be used because they burn easily.

6. Make sure to stir any mixtures containing cornstarch immediately before using to prevent lumps.

7. Heat the skillet or wok first, then add the oil. Make sure the oil is hot before adding any food. The oil is hot enough if a piece of vegetable sizzles when tossed into the pan.

8. Keep the food in constant motion, tossing and stirring it with a flat metal or wooden spatula. This prevents it from burning and also seals in the flavor.

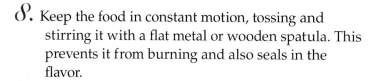

Slow Cooker Cooking

Slow cookers were introduced in the 1970's; their popularity was renewed in the mid-1990's and continues into the present day. Considering the hectic pace of today's lifestyles, it's no wonder so many people have rediscovered this time-saving kitchen appliance. Spend a few minutes preparing the ingredients, or buy precut meat and vegetables, so all you have to do is place them right in the slow cooker and relax. The low heat and long cooking times take the stress out of meal preparation. Leave for work or a day of leisure and come home to a hot, delicious meal.

There are two types of slow cookers. The most common models have heat coils circling the crockery inset, allowing heat to surround the food and cook evenly. Two settings, LOW (about 200°F) and HIGH (about 300°F) regulate cooking temperatures. One hour on HIGH equals 2 to 2½ hours on LOW. Less common models have heat coils on the bottom. If you own this type, consult your manufacturer's instructions for advice on converting the recipes in this publication.

Selecting Meat

Keep in mind that you can, and in fact should, use tougher, inexpensive cuts of meat. Top-quality cuts, such as loin chops or filet mignon, fall apart during long cooking periods and therefore are not good choices to use in the slow cooker. You will be amazed to find that even the toughest cuts of meat will come out fork-tender and flavorful.

Cutting Vegetables

Vegetables often take longer to cook than meats. Cut vegetables into small, thin, uniformly sized pieces and place them near the bottom or side of the slow cooker. Pay careful attention to the recipe instructions in order to cut vegetables to the proper size so they will cook in the amount of time given.

Converting Recipes

If you would like to adapt your own recipe to cook in a slow cooker, you'll need to follow a few guidelines. First, try to find a similar slow cooker recipe. Take note of the cooking times, amount of liquid, and quantity and size of meat and vegetable pieces. The slow cooker captures moisture, so you will want to reduce the amount of liquid in the original recipe, often by as much as half.

Quick Tips for the Slow Cooker

- Manufacturers recommend that slow cookers should be one-half to three-quarters full for the best results.

- To make cleanup easier, spray the inside of the slow cooker with nonstick cooking spray before adding any food.

- Cooking times are guidelines. Slow cookers, just like ovens, cook differently depending on heating units. The cooking times may need to be adjusted slightly.

- Keep a lid on it! A slow cooker can take as long as twenty minutes to regain heat lost when the cover is removed. If the recipe calls for stirring or checking the dish near the end of the cooking time, replace the cover as quickly as you can. Otherwise, resist the urge to remove the cover. Only remove it when instructed to do so in the recipe.

- Spinning the cover until the condensation falls off will allow you to see inside the slow cooker without removing the lid, which delays the cooking time.

- Slow cooker recipes with raw meats should cook a minimum of 3 hours on LOW for food safety reasons.

- Do not cook whole chickens in the slow cooker because the temperature of the chicken cannot reach the desired level quickly enough for food safety. Cut a whole chicken into quarters or parts.

- Dairy products should be added at the end of the cooking time because they will curdle if cooked in the slow cooker for a long time.

- Always taste the finished dish before serving it. Seasonings often need to be adjusted to your preferences.

Foil to the Rescue

To easily lift a dish out of the slow cooker, make foil handles following the directions below.

- Tear off three 18×3-inch strips of heavy-duty foil. Crisscross the strips so they resemble the spokes of a wheel. Place your dish in the center of the strips.

- Pull the foil strips up and place the dish into the slow cooker. Leave the strips in while you cook so you can easily lift the dish out again when ready.

Pantry Provisions

Here's a basic list of pantry staples that should be part of every one-dish cook's kitchen. As with one-dish meals themselves, the list should be adjusted to suit you and your family's individual tastes.

Grains and Pasta: pasta, including long spaghetti types, shorter macaroni types, egg noodles and lasagna noodles; rice (white, brown and/or wild, flavored rice mixes, arborio rice for risotto)

Canned Goods: beans (black, kidney, white); broth and bouillon; chicken, ham or corned beef; condensed soup; olives; pasta sauces; tomato sauce and tomato paste; tomatoes (whole, stewed and diced with flavorings); tuna

Condiments: hot sauce; ketchup and barbecue sauce; mayonnaise; mustard; olive and vegetable oil; sour cream or yogurt; soy sauce; vinegar (white, balsamic, wine or cider); Worcestershire sauce

Dry Goods: biscuit baking mix; bread crumbs; cornmeal; cereal; all-purpose flour; nuts; stuffing mix

Vegetables and Fruit: frozen vegetables; garlic; lemons and limes; onions; potatoes

Chili Relleno Casserole

1½ cups (6 ounces) SARGENTO® Reduced Fat
    4 Cheese Mexican Shredded Cheese,
    divided
1 can (12 ounces) evaporated skim milk
¾ cup (6 ounces) fat-free liquid egg substitute
    or 3 eggs, beaten
6 (7-inch) corn tortillas, torn into 2-inch
    pieces
2 cans (4 ounces each) chopped green chilies
½ cup mild chunky salsa
¼ teaspoon salt (optional)
2 tablespoons chopped fresh cilantro
   Light or fat-free sour cream (optional)

1. Coat 10-inch deep-dish pie plate or 8-inch
square baking dish with nonstick cooking spray.
In medium bowl, combine 1 cup cheese, milk,
egg substitute, tortillas, chilies, salsa and salt,
if desired. Mix well; pour into prepared dish.

2. Bake at 375°F 35 minutes or until set. Remove
from oven; sprinkle with remaining ½ cup cheese
and cilantro. Return to oven; bake 1 minute or
until cheese is melted. Serve with sour cream, if
desired.   *Makes 4 servings*

Chili Relleno Casserole

Linguine Frittata

8 ounces uncooked linguine
3 tablespoons olive oil, divided
1 cup chopped carrots
¼ cup chopped onion
2 cloves garlic, minced
½ pound asparagus, cut into 1-inch pieces
1 large red bell pepper, diced
1 medium tomato, seeded and chopped
1 teaspoon dried basil
1 teaspoon dried marjoram
1 teaspoon dried oregano
5 eggs
¼ cup grated Parmesan cheese
½ teaspoon salt
¼ teaspoon black pepper

1. Cook linguine according to package directions. Drain in colander. Place in large bowl.

2. Heat 1 tablespoon oil in large skillet over medium heat until hot. Add carrots, onion and garlic; cook and stir 5 minutes or until carrots are crisp-tender. Add asparagus, bell pepper, tomato, basil, marjoram and oregano; cook and stir 5 minutes or until asparagus is crisp-tender. Add vegetable mixture to linguine in bowl; mix well.

3. Beat eggs in medium bowl with wire whisk until frothy. Stir in cheese, salt and black pepper; pour over linguine mixture and toss.

4. Heat remaining 2 tablespoons oil in 12-inch nonstick skillet over medium heat until hot. Add linguine mixture, spreading evenly. Reduce heat to low. Cook 5 minutes or until browned on bottom. Place large rimless plate over skillet; invert frittata onto plate. Slide frittata back into skillet. Cook 5 minutes more or until browned on bottom and eggs are set. Slide frittata onto serving plate. Cut into wedges. *Makes 6 to 8 servings*

Linguine Frittata

Pizza for Breakfast

1 (6½-ounce) package pizza crust mix
1 pound BOB EVANS® Original Recipe Roll Sausage
1 cup diced fresh or drained canned tomatoes
8 ounces fresh mushrooms, sliced
1½ cups (6 ounces) shredded mozzarella cheese, divided
1½ cups (6 ounces) shredded sharp Cheddar cheese, divided
4 eggs
 Salt and black pepper to taste
 Salsa (optional)

Preheat oven to 350°F. Prepare crust mix according to package directions. Spread pizza dough into greased 13×9-inch baking dish, making sure dough evenly covers bottom and 2 inches up sides of dish. Crumble and cook sausage in medium skillet until browned; drain well on paper towels. Top crust with sausage, tomatoes, mushrooms, 1 cup mozzarella cheese and 1 cup Cheddar cheese. Bake 8 to 10 minutes or until crust is golden brown at edges. Remove from oven. Whisk eggs, salt and pepper in small bowl; pour over pizza. Return to oven; bake 7 to 9 minutes more or until eggs are set. Immediately sprinkle with remaining cheeses. Serve hot with salsa, if desired. Refrigerate leftovers.

Makes 8 to 10 servings

Note: Refrigerated crescent roll dough may be used instead of pizza crust mix. Seal edges together and stretch to fit baking dish.

Recently there has been an explosion of mushrooms in the marketplace. In fancy produce stores you can now find many varieties of mushrooms—cepes, chanterelles, enoki, morels, shiitake and porcini, to name just a few. The domestic white button mushroom, however, continues to be the most popular and widely available. Choose button mushrooms that have caps tightly closed around the stems; the dark interior of the caps should not be showing.

Surimi Seafood-Zucchini Frittata with Fresh Tomato Sauce

2 tablespoons vegetable oil
1 zucchini, thinly sliced
½ cup chopped onion
¼ cup chopped green bell pepper
3 eggs
6 egg whites
2 teaspoons finely chopped fresh basil *or* ½ teaspoon dried basil
½ teaspoon salt, optional
¼ teaspoon black pepper
6 ounces crab or lobster-flavored surimi seafood, chunk style
2 tablespoons butter or margarine
3 cups chunky tomato sauce

Preheat oven to 375°F. Heat oil in 10-inch heavy ovenproof skillet over medium heat. Add zucchini, onion and green pepper; cook 5 minutes, stirring often. Place in medium bowl; set aside to cool slightly. In large bowl, beat eggs and egg whites with basil, salt and pepper until well blended. Add zucchini mixture and surimi seafood; stir well. Meanwhile, melt butter in same skillet over medium heat, swirling skillet to coat evenly with butter. Pour in egg-surimi seafood mixture and place skillet on middle shelf of oven. Bake 12 to 15 minutes, or until eggs are set throughout. Loosen around edges with metal spatula; cut into wedges. Serve hot with ½ cup tomato sauce over each frittata slice. *Makes 6 servings*

Favorite recipe from **National Fisheries Institute**

Surimi Seafood-Zucchini Frittata with Fresh Tomato Sauce

Classic Spinach Soufflé

 1 pound fresh spinach leaves
¼ cup (½ stick) butter
 2 tablespoons finely chopped onion
¼ cup all-purpose flour
¼ teaspoon salt
¼ teaspoon ground nutmeg
⅛ teaspoon black pepper
 1 cup milk
 4 eggs, separated
 1 cup (4 ounces) shredded sharp Cheddar cheese

1. Preheat oven to 375° F. Grease 1½- or 2-quart soufflé dish; set aside.

2. Bring 1 quart salted water in 2-quart saucepan to a boil over high heat. Add spinach. Return to a boil and cook 2 to 3 minutes or until spinach is crisp-tender. Drain spinach and immediately plunge into cold water. Drain again; let stand until cool enough to handle. Squeeze spinach to remove excess moisture. Finely chop spinach.

3. Melt butter in large saucepan over medium heat. Add onion; cook and stir 2 to 3 minutes. Stir in flour, salt, nutmeg and pepper. Gradually stir in milk. Cook and stir until mixture comes to a boil and thickens. Remove from heat.

4. Stir egg yolks into saucepan until well blended. Add spinach and cheese; mix well.

5. Beat egg whites in clean large bowl with electric mixer at high speed until stiff peaks form. Fold egg whites into spinach mixture until egg whites are evenly incorporated. Pour into prepared dish.

6. Bake 35 to 40 minutes or until puffed and wooden skewer inserted in center comes out clean. Garnish, if desired. Serve immediately.   *Makes 4 servings*

Classic Spinach Soufflé

Caribbean Brunch Strata

6 BAYS® English Muffins, halved, split
1 tablespoon Caribbean jerk seasoning (sweet and spicy)
1 whole boneless, skinless chicken breast* (about 8 ounces), cut into ½-inch pieces
1 tablespoon oil
¼ cup sliced green onions with tops
3 tablespoons flaked or shredded coconut
4 ounces mild goat cheese, crumbled
6 eggs
3¾ cups milk
¼ to ½ teaspoon liquid red pepper seasoning
½ teaspoon salt
Mango Salsa (recipe follows)

One-half pound peeled, deveined medium shrimp can be substituted for chicken.

Preheat oven to 325°F. Arrange half of English muffin pieces on the bottom of a buttered 2-quart glass casserole. Sprinkle jerk seasoning on chicken; toss to coat evenly. In a large skillet, heat oil over medium heat. Add chicken; cook and stir until firm, 3 to 5 minutes. Spoon over muffins. Sprinkle with green onions, coconut and cheese. Top with remaining muffin pieces. Beat eggs, milk, pepper seasoning and salt together until blended. Spoon mixture over muffins. Cover with plastic wrap; refrigerate several hours or overnight. When ready to bake, remove plastic. Bake 50 to 60 minutes, until puffy and brown. If necessary, cover with foil during the last 10 minutes of baking to prevent over-browning. Serve with Mango Salsa and tossed green salad.   *Makes 4 servings*

Mango Salsa

1 medium mango, peeled, pitted and finely chopped (1 cup)
1 red boiling onion, peeled, thinly sliced
1 tablespoon snipped fresh parsley or cilantro
1 teaspoon minced serrano or jalapeño pepper,** seeded and deveined
¼ teaspoon freshly grated lime peel
Salt and black pepper to taste
1 to 2 tablespoons lime juice, to taste

**Chili peppers can sting and irritate the skin, so wear rubber gloves when handling peppers and do not touch your eyes.*

Mix all ingredients. Cover; refrigerate to blend flavors.   *Makes 1 cup salsa*

Caribbean Brunch Strata

❧ Eggs ❧

Ham and Swiss Quiche

1 cup (4 ounces) shredded Swiss cheese, *divided*
1 cup finely chopped cooked ham
2 green onions, sliced
1 *unbaked* 9-inch (4-cup volume) deep-dish pie shell
1 can (12 fluid ounces) NESTLÉ® CARNATION® Evaporated Milk
3 large eggs
¼ cup all-purpose flour
¼ teaspoon salt
⅛ teaspoon ground black pepper

PREHEAT oven to 350°F.

SPRINKLE *½ cup* cheese, ham and green onions into pie crust. Whisk together evaporated milk, eggs, flour, salt and pepper in large bowl. Pour mixture into pie shell; sprinkle with *remaining* cheese.

BAKE for 45 to 50 minutes or until knife inserted near center comes out clean. Cool on wire rack for 10 minutes before serving.   *Makes 8 servings*

For Mini-Quiche Appetizers: Use 1½ packages (3 crusts) refrigerated pie crusts. Grease miniature muffin pans. Unfold crust on lightly floured surface. Cut fourteen 2½-inch circles from each crust. Press 1 circle of dough onto bottom and up side of each cup. Repeat with *remaining* crusts. Combine cheese, ham, green onions, *⅔ cup (5-fluid-ounce can)* evaporated milk, 2 eggs (lightly beaten), *2 tablespoons* flour, salt and pepper in large bowl; mix well. Spoon mixture into crusts, filling ¾ full. Bake in preheated 350°F. oven for 20 to 25 minutes or until crusts are golden brown. Cool slightly; lift quiches from cups with tip of knife. Serve warm or cool and freeze for later entertaining. Makes 3½ dozen appetizers.

Artichoke Frittata

1 can (14 ounces) artichoke hearts, drained
3 teaspoons olive oil, divided
½ cup minced green onions
5 eggs
½ cup (2 ounces) shredded Swiss cheese
2 tablespoons grated Parmesan cheese
1 tablespoon minced fresh parsley
1 teaspoon salt
   Black pepper

1. Chop artichoke hearts; set aside.

2. Heat 2 teaspoons oil in 10-inch skillet over medium heat. Add green onions; cook and stir until tender. Remove from skillet.

3. Beat eggs in medium bowl until light. Stir in artichokes, green onions, cheeses, parsley, salt and pepper to taste.

4. Heat remaining 1 teaspoon oil in same skillet over medium heat. Pour egg mixture into skillet. Cook 4 to 5 minutes or until bottom is lightly browned. Place large plate over skillet; invert frittata onto plate. Return frittata, uncooked side down, to skillet. Cook about 4 minutes more or until center is just set. Cut into wedges. *Makes 6 servings*

Mincing refers to the technique of chopping food into very tiny, irregular pieces. Minced food is smaller than chopped food. Flavorful seasonings, such as garlic and fresh herbs, are often minced to distribute their flavor more evenly throughout a dish.

Cranberry Sausage Quiche

    1 (9-inch) frozen deep-dish pie shell
    ½ pound BOB EVANS® Savory Sage Roll Sausage
    ¼ cup chopped yellow onion
    ¾ cup dried cranberries
    1½ cups (6 ounces) shredded Monterey Jack cheese
    3 eggs, lightly beaten
    1½ cups half-and-half
    Fresh parsley or sage leaves for garnish

Preheat oven to 400°F. Let frozen pie shell stand at room temperature 10 minutes; do not prick shell. Bake 7 minutes. Remove from oven and set aside. Reduce oven temperature to 375°F. Crumble and cook sausage and onion in large skillet over medium-high heat until sausage is browned. Remove from heat and drain off any drippings. Stir in cranberries. Sprinkle cheese on bottom of pie shell; top evenly with sausage mixture. Combine eggs and half-and-half in medium bowl; whisk until blended but not frothy. Pour egg mixture over sausage mixture in pie shell. Bake 40 to 45 minutes or until knife inserted into center comes out clean. Let stand 10 minutes before serving. Garnish with fresh parsley. Refrigerate leftovers.   *Makes 6 servings*

Spinach Pie

    1 tablespoon FILIPPO BERIO® Olive Oil
    1 pound fresh spinach, washed, drained and stems removed
    1 medium potato, cooked and mashed
    2 eggs, beaten
    ¼ cup cottage cheese
    2 tablespoons grated Romano cheese
    Salt

Preheat oven to 350°F. Grease 8-inch round cake pan with olive oil. Tear spinach into bite-size pieces. In large bowl, combine spinach, potato, eggs, cottage cheese and Romano cheese. Spoon mixture into prepared pan. Bake 15 to 20 minutes or until set. Season to taste with salt.   *Makes 6 servings*

Cranberry Sausage Quiche

Bacon and Maple Grits Puff

    8 slices bacon
    2 cups milk
1¼ cups water
    1 cup uncooked quick-cooking grits
    ½ teaspoon salt
    ½ cup pure maple syrup
    4 eggs
       Fresh chives (optional)

1. Preheat oven to 350°F. Grease 1½-quart round casserole or soufflé dish; set aside.

2. Cook bacon in large skillet over medium-high heat about 7 minutes or until crisp. Remove bacon to paper towels; set aside. Reserve 2 tablespoons bacon drippings.

3. Combine milk, water, grits and salt in medium saucepan. Bring to a boil over medium heat, stirring frequently. Simmer 2 to 3 minutes or until mixture thickens, stirring constantly. Remove from heat; stir in syrup and reserved 2 tablespoons bacon drippings.

4. Crumble bacon; reserve ¼ cup for garnish. Stir remaining crumbled bacon into grits mixture.

5. Beat eggs in medium bowl. Gradually stir small amount of grits mixture into eggs. Stir egg mixture into remaining grits mixture. Pour into prepared casserole.

6. Bake 1 hour 20 minutes or until knife inserted into center comes out clean. Top with reserved ¼ cup bacon. Garnish with fresh chives. Serve immediately.

Makes 6 to 8 servings

Note: Puff will fall slightly after being removed from oven.

Bacon and Maple Grits Puff

Hash Brown Casserole

6 eggs, well beaten
1 can (12 fluid ounces) NESTLÉ® CARNATION® Evaporated Milk
1 teaspoon salt
½ teaspoon ground black pepper
1 package (30 ounces) frozen shredded hash brown potatoes
2 cups (8 ounces) shredded cheddar cheese
1 medium onion, chopped
1 small green bell pepper, chopped
1 cup diced ham (optional)

PREHEAT oven to 350°F. Grease 13×9-inch baking dish.

COMBINE eggs, evaporated milk, salt and black pepper in large bowl. Add potatoes, cheese, onion, bell pepper and ham, if desired; mix well. Pour mixture into prepared baking dish.

BAKE for 60 to 65 minutes or until set.   *Makes 12 servings*

Note: For a lower fat version of this recipe, substitute 3 cartons (4 ounces *each*) cholesterol-free egg product for the eggs, NESTLÉ® CARNATION® Evaporated Fat Free Milk for Evaporated Milk, and 10 slices turkey bacon, cooked and chopped, for the diced ham. Proceed as above.

Evaporated milk, not to be confused with sweetened condensed milk, is homogenized milk which has had 60% of its water removed. Sweeteners are not added. Evaporated milk comes in cans and is available made with whole, low-fat and fat-free milk.

Hash Brown Casserole

Feta Brunch Bake

1 medium red bell pepper
2 bags (10 ounces each) fresh spinach, washed and stemmed
6 eggs
6 ounces crumbled feta cheese
⅓ cup chopped onion
2 tablespoons chopped fresh parsley
¼ teaspoon dried dill weed
  Dash black pepper

1. Preheat broiler. Place bell pepper on foil-lined broiler pan. Broil, 4 inches from heat, 15 to 20 minutes or until blackened on all sides, turning every 5 minutes with tongs. Place in paper bag; close bag and set aside to cool about 15 to 20 minutes. To peel pepper, cut around core, twist and remove. Cut in half and rub off skin; rinse under cold water. Cut into ½-inch pieces.

2. To blanch spinach, place 1 quart water in 2-quart saucepan over high heat; bring to a boil. Add spinach. Return to a boil; boil 2 to 3 minutes or until crisp-tender. Drain; immediately plunge spinach into cold water. Drain; let stand until cool enough to handle. Squeeze spinach to remove excess water; finely chop.

3. Preheat oven to 400°F. Grease 1-quart baking dish. Beat eggs in large bowl with electric mixer at medium speed until foamy. Stir in bell pepper, spinach, cheese, onion, parsley, dill weed and black pepper. Pour egg mixture into prepared dish. Bake 20 minutes or until set. Let stand 5 minutes before serving. Garnish as desired. *Makes 4 servings*

Feta Brunch Bake

Eggs

33

Parmesan and Roasted Red Pepper Strata

1 loaf (16 ounces) French bread, cut into ½-inch-thick slices
2 jars (7½ ounces each) roasted red peppers, drained and cut into ½-inch
    pieces
1 cup grated Parmesan cheese
1 cup sliced green onions
3 cups (12 ounces) shredded mozzarella cheese
8 eggs
¾ cup milk
1 container (7 ounces) prepared pesto
2 teaspoons minced garlic
¾ teaspoon salt

1. Grease 13×9-inch baking dish. Arrange half of bread slices in single layer on bottom of prepared baking dish. Top bread with half of red peppers, ½ cup Parmesan, ½ cup green onions and 1½ cups mozzarella. Repeat layers with remaining bread, red peppers, Parmesan, green onions and mozzarella.

2. Combine eggs, milk, pesto, garlic and salt in medium bowl; whisk until blended. Pour egg mixture evenly over strata. Cover and refrigerate overnight.

3. Preheat oven to 375°F. Bake, uncovered, 30 minutes or until hot and bubbly.

Makes 6 servings

Note: If time allows, let the strata stand at room temperature for about 15 minutes before baking.

Cheesy Country SPAM™ *Puff*

6 slices white bread, torn into small pieces
1¼ cups milk
3 eggs
1 tablespoon spicy mustard
½ teaspoon garlic powder
½ teaspoon paprika
1 (12-ounce) can SPAM® Classic, cubed
2 cups (8 ounces) shredded sharp Cheddar cheese, divided
½ cup chopped onion
½ cup (2 ounces) shredded Monterey Jack cheese

Heat oven to 375°F. In large bowl, combine bread, milk, eggs, mustard, garlic powder and paprika. Beat at medium speed of electric mixer 1 minute or until smooth. Stir in SPAM®, 1 cup Cheddar cheese and onion. Pour into greased 12×8-inch baking dish. Bake 25 minutes. Top with remaining 1 cup Cheddar cheese and Monterey Jack cheese. Bake 5 minutes longer or until cheese is melted. Let stand 10 minutes before serving. *Makes 8 servings*

Summer Quiche

6 eggs
¾ cup plain STONYFIELD FARM® Yogurt
½ tablespoon chopped fresh basil
½ tablespoon chopped fresh thyme
¼ teaspoon black pepper
2 tablespoons grated Parmesan cheese
3 Roma tomatoes, diced
1 small yellow squash, diced
1 small zucchini, diced
1 small Vidalia onion, diced
1 unbaked 9-inch pie shell

Preheat oven to 375°F. In large bowl, combine eggs, yogurt, herbs, pepper and Parmesan cheese. Beat well. Add tomatoes, yellow squash, zucchini and onion; stir. Pour mixture into pie shell; bake for 35 to 45 minutes or until cooked through (quiche should be firm to the touch). Let cool for 10 minutes before serving. *Makes 6 to 8 servings*

Cheesy Country SPAM™ *Puff*

Italian Alfredo Broccoli Strata

1 loaf (12 ounces) Italian bread, cut into 1-inch cubes
1 jar (1 pound) RAGÚ® Cheesy! Classic Alfredo Sauce
3 cups milk
6 eggs, lightly beaten
1½ cups shredded mozzarella cheese (about 6 ounces)
1 box (10 ounces) frozen chopped broccoli, thawed and drained

1. Preheat oven to 350°F. In greased 13×9-inch baking dish, arrange bread cubes; set aside.

2. In large bowl with wire whisk, combine remaining ingredients; pour over bread. Let stand 1 hour or cover and refrigerate overnight.

3. Bake uncovered, 45 minutes or until center is set.   *Makes 6 servings*

Prep Time: 15 minutes
Stand Time: 1 hour
Cook Time: 45 minutes

Variation: For a meat variation, add 1 cup coarsely diced cooked ham, 1 cup crumbled cooked sausage or 6 slices bacon, cooked and crumbled.

Crustless Crab Florentine Quiche

1 can (6 ounces) crabmeat, well drained and flaked
½ package (10 ounces) frozen chopped spinach, thawed and well drained
½ cup chopped onion
1 cup fat-free shredded Cheddar cheese
4 SAUDER'S® large egg whites
2 SAUDER'S® large eggs
1 can (12 ounces) evaporated low-fat milk
½ teaspoon salt-free herb and spice blend

Line bottom of quiche dish or 9-inch pie plate with crabmeat. Top with spinach, onion and cheese. Blend egg whites, eggs, milk and spice blend. Pour over crabmeat mixture. Bake at 350°F for 45 minutes. Allow to stand 10 minutes before serving.   *Makes 4 to 6 servings*

Note: Canned crab is available as lump, claw meat or flaked. Once opened, keep canned crabmeat refrigerated and use within two days.

Aunt Marilyn's Cinnamon French Toast Casserole

1 large loaf French bread, cut into 1½-inch slices
3½ cups milk
9 eggs
1½ cups sugar, divided
1 tablespoon vanilla
½ teaspoon salt
6 to 8 medium baking apples, such as McIntosh or Cortland, peeled and sliced
1 teaspoon ground cinnamon
½ teaspoon ground nutmeg

1. Place bread slices in greased 13×9-inch glass baking dish or casserole.

2. Combine milk, eggs, 1 cup sugar, vanilla and salt in large bowl; whisk until well blended. Pour half of mixture over bread.

3. Layer apple slices over bread. Pour remaining half of egg mixture over apples.

4. Combine remaining ½ cup sugar, cinnamon and nutmeg in small bowl; sprinkle over casserole. Cover and refrigerate overnight.

5. Preheat oven to 350°F. Bake, uncovered, 1 hour or until set.

Makes 6 to 8 servings

Apples will keep in a cool, dry place for a week or two. For longer storage, place apples in a plastic bag and store them in the refrigerator. Apples in good condition can last up to six weeks in the refrigerator. Check them occasionally and discard any that have begun to spoil, as one rotten apple can ruin the whole lot.

Greek Spinach and Feta Pie

⅓ cup butter, melted
2 eggs
1 package (10 ounces) frozen chopped spinach, thawed and squeezed dry
1 container (15 ounces) ricotta cheese
1 package (4 ounces) crumbled feta cheese
¾ teaspoon finely grated lemon peel
¼ teaspoon black pepper
⅛ teaspoon ground nutmeg
1 package (16 ounces) frozen phyllo dough, thawed

1. Preheat oven to 350°F. Brush 13×9-inch baking dish lightly with butter.

2. Beat eggs in medium bowl. Stir in spinach, ricotta, feta, lemon peel, pepper and nutmeg. Set aside.

3. Unwrap phyllo dough; remove 8 sheets. Cut dough in half crosswise forming 16 rectangles about 13×8½ inches. Cover dough with damp cloth or plastic wrap to keep moist while assembling pie. Reserve remaining dough for another use.

4. Place 1 piece of dough in prepared dish; brush top lightly with butter. Layer with another piece of dough and brush lightly with butter. Continue layering with 6 pieces of dough, brushing each lightly with butter. Spoon spinach mixture evenly over dough.

5. Top spinach mixture with piece of dough; brush lightly with butter. Repeat layering with remaining 7 pieces of dough, brushing each piece lightly with butter.

6. Bake, uncovered, 35 to 40 minutes or until golden brown.

Makes 6 servings

Greek Spinach and Feta Pie

Barley, Bean and Corn Frittata

2 cups water
½ cup barley
¾ teaspoon salt, divided
2 teaspoons olive oil
1 can (15 ounces) black beans, drained and rinsed
2 cups (8 ounces) shredded Cheddar cheese, divided
¾ cup fresh cut corn*
½ cup chopped green bell pepper
¼ cup chopped fresh cilantro
7 eggs *or* 1¾ cups cholesterol-free egg substitute
1 cup cottage cheese
½ teaspoon ground red pepper
1 cup medium salsa
Sour cream (optional)

Frozen corn can be substituted for fresh; thaw before using.

1. Bring water to a boil in medium saucepan over high heat. Add barley and ¼ teaspoon salt. Reduce heat to low. Cover and simmer 40 to 45 minutes or until tender. Let stand, covered, 5 minutes. Drain.

2. Preheat oven to 400°F. Brush 10-inch cast iron or ovenproof skillet with olive oil. Layer barley, beans, 1 cup Cheddar cheese, corn, bell pepper and cilantro in skillet. Blend eggs, cottage cheese, remaining ½ teaspoon salt and ground red pepper in blender or food processor just until smooth. Carefully pour egg mixture over layers.

3. Bake 30 minutes or until egg mixture is set. Sprinkle with remaining 1 cup Cheddar cheese. Bake 5 minutes or until cheese is melted. Spoon salsa evenly over top. Let stand 5 minutes before cutting into wedges. Garnish with sour cream.
Makes 6 to 8 servings

Barley, Bean and Corn Frittata

Make-Ahead Breakfast Casserole

2½ cups seasoned croutons
1 pound BOB EVANS® Original Recipe Roll Sausage
2¼ cups milk
4 eggs
1 (10½-ounce) can condensed cream of mushroom soup, undiluted
1 (10-ounce) package frozen chopped spinach, thawed and squeezed dry
1 (4-ounce) can mushrooms, drained and chopped
1 cup (4 ounces) shredded sharp Cheddar cheese
1 cup (4 ounces) shredded Monterey Jack cheese
¼ teaspoon dry mustard
Fresh herb sprigs and carrot strips (optional)
Picante sauce or salsa (optional)

Spread croutons on bottom of greased 13×9-inch baking dish. Crumble sausage into medium skillet. Cook over medium heat until browned, stirring occasionally. Drain off any drippings. Spread over croutons. Whisk milk and eggs in large bowl until blended. Stir in soup, spinach, mushrooms, cheeses and mustard. Pour egg mixture over sausage and croutons. Refrigerate overnight. Preheat oven to 325°F. Bake egg mixture 50 to 55 minutes or until set and lightly browned on top. Garnish with herb sprigs and carrot strips, if desired. Serve hot with picante sauce, if desired. Refrigerate leftovers.

Makes 10 to 12 servings

Make-Ahead Breakfast Casserole

Ham and Egg Enchiladas

      2 tablespoons butter
      1 small red bell pepper, chopped
      3 green onions with tops, sliced
      ½ cup diced ham
      8 eggs
      8 (7- to 8-inch) flour tortillas
      ½ cup (2 ounces) shredded pepper jack cheese
      1 can (10 ounces) enchilada sauce
      ½ cup prepared salsa
      1½ cups (6 ounces) shredded pepper jack cheese (optional)

1. Preheat oven to 350°F.

2. Melt butter in large nonstick skillet over medium heat. Add bell pepper and onions; cook and stir 2 minutes. Add ham; cook and stir 1 minute.

3. Lightly beat eggs with wire whisk in medium bowl. Add eggs to skillet; cook until eggs are set but still soft, stirring occasionally.

4. Spoon about ⅓ cup egg mixture evenly down center of each tortilla; top with 1 tablespoon cheese. Roll tortillas up and place seam side down in shallow 11×7-inch baking dish.

5. Combine enchilada sauce and salsa in small bowl; pour evenly over enchiladas.

6. Cover enchiladas with foil; bake 20 minutes. Uncover; sprinkle with 1½ cups cheese, if desired. Continue baking 10 minutes or until enchiladas are hot and cheese is melted. Garnish as desired. Serve immediately.

Makes 4 servings

Ham and Egg Enchiladas

Sausage Vegetable Frittata

5 eggs
¼ cup milk
2 tablespoons grated Parmesan cheese
½ teaspoon dried oregano leaves
½ teaspoon black pepper
1 (10-ounce) package BOB EVANS® Skinless Link Sausage
2 tablespoons butter or margarine
1 small zucchini, sliced (about 1 cup)
½ cup shredded carrots
⅓ cup sliced green onions with tops
¾ cup (3 ounces) shredded Swiss cheese
Carrot curls (optional)

Whisk eggs in medium bowl; stir in milk, Parmesan cheese, oregano and pepper. Set aside. Cook sausage in large skillet over medium heat until browned, turning occasionally. Drain off any drippings. Remove sausage from skillet and cut into ½-inch pieces. Melt butter in same skillet. Add zucchini, shredded carrots and onions; cook and stir over medium heat until tender. Top with sausage, then Swiss cheese. Pour egg mixture over vegetable mixture. Stir gently to combine. Cook, without stirring, over low heat 8 to 10 minutes or until center is almost set. Remove from heat. Let stand 5 minutes before cutting into wedges; serve hot. Garnish with carrot curls, if desired. Refrigerate leftovers.

Makes 4 to 6 servings

Chili Cheese Puff

¾ **cup all-purpose flour**
1½ **teaspoons baking powder**
9 **eggs**
4 **cups (16 ounces) shredded Monterey Jack cheese**
2 **cups (16 ounces) 1% low-fat cottage cheese**
2 **cans (4 ounces each) diced green chilies, drained**
1½ **teaspoons sugar**
¼ **teaspoon salt**
⅛ **teaspoon hot pepper sauce**
1 **cup prepared salsa**

1. Preheat oven to 350°F. Spray 13×9-inch baking dish with nonstick cooking spray.

2. Combine flour and baking powder in small bowl.

3. Whisk eggs in large bowl until blended; stir in Monterey Jack, cottage cheese, chilies, sugar, salt and hot pepper sauce. Add flour mixture; stir just until blended. Pour into prepared dish.

4. Bake, uncovered, 45 minutes or until set. Let stand 5 minutes before serving. Serve with salsa.

Makes 8 servings

Refrigerate eggs immediately after purchasing. To prevent them from absorbing odors from other foods, store them in the original carton. For best flavor, use eggs within a week after purchasing. However, they will keep for five weeks after the packing date without loss of nutrients.

Chili Cheese Puff

Tamale Potato Quiche

½ pound small red potatoes, peeled and sliced ⅛ inch thick
1 cup white cornmeal
1 teaspoon ground cumin
¾ teaspoon salt, divided
2 cups (8 ounces) shredded Cheddar cheese, divided
4 eggs, divided
⅓ cup water
2 tablespoons olive oil
½ cup cottage cheese
2 tablespoons milk
¼ teaspoon black pepper
1 can (4 ounces) chopped green chiles, drained
1 medium red bell pepper, seeded and cut into thin strips
Sour cream and fresh cilantro

1. Place potatoes in small saucepan; cover with water. Bring to a boil over high heat. Reduce heat to low. Cover and simmer 5 minutes or until potatoes are crisp-tender. Drain. Set aside.

2. Combine cornmeal, cumin, ¼ teaspoon salt and 1 cup Cheddar cheese in medium bowl; toss to mix. Beat 1 egg in small bowl; beat in water and oil until blended. Stir into cornmeal mixture just until cornmeal is moistened.

3. Pat mixture evenly on bottom and up side of greased 9-inch glass pie plate.

4. Place remaining 3 eggs, cottage cheese, milk, remaining ½ teaspoon salt and black pepper in blender; process until smooth.

5. Arrange half of potatoes in layer in crust. Sprinkle with green chiles and ½ cup Cheddar cheese. Top with remaining potatoes and ½ cup Cheddar cheese. Arrange bell pepper strips on top. Carefully pour egg mixture over layers, allowing mixture to seep through layers.

6. Cover completely with plastic wrap, folding ends under. Place round metal cooling rack inside wok; fill wok with 1½ inches water. (Water should not touch rack.) Place pie plate on rack. Bring water to a boil over high heat; reduce heat to low. Cover wok; steam 35 to 40 minutes or until egg mixture is set. (Replenish water, if necessary.)

7. Cool 10 minutes. Cut into wedges. Garnish with sour cream and cilantro.

Makes 6 servings

Tamale Potato Quiche

Farmstand Frittata

    Nonstick cooking spray
 1 medium red bell pepper, seeded and cut into thin strips
 ½ cup chopped onion
 1 cup broccoli florets, blanched and drained
 1 cup cooked quartered unpeeled red potatoes
 1 cup cholesterol-free egg substitute
 6 egg whites
 1 tablespoon chopped fresh parsley
 ½ teaspoon salt
 ¼ teaspoon black pepper
 ½ cup (2 ounces) shredded Cheddar cheese

1. Spray large nonstick ovenproof skillet with cooking spray; heat over medium heat until hot. Add bell pepper and onion; cook and stir 3 minutes or until crisp-tender.

2. Add broccoli and potatoes; cook and stir 1 to 2 minutes or until heated through.

3. Whisk together egg substitute, egg whites, parsley, salt and black pepper in medium bowl.

4. Spread vegetables in even layer in skillet. Pour egg white mixture over vegetables; cover and cook over medium heat 10 to 12 minutes or until egg mixture is set.

5. Meanwhile, preheat broiler. Top frittata with cheese. Broil 4 inches from heat 1 minute or until cheese is melted. Cut into 4 wedges to serve. Garnish as desired.

Makes 4 servings

Artichoke-Olive Chicken Bake

1½ cups uncooked rotini pasta
1 tablespoon olive oil
1 medium onion, chopped
½ green bell pepper, chopped
2 cups shredded cooked chicken
1 can (about 14 ounces) diced tomatoes with Italian-style herbs
1 can (14 ounces) artichoke hearts, drained and quartered
1 can (6 ounces) sliced black olives, drained
1 teaspoon Italian seasoning
2 cups (8 ounces) shredded mozzarella cheese

1. Preheat oven to 350°F. Spray 2-quart casserole with nonstick cooking spray.

2. Cook pasta according to package directions until al dente. Drain.

3. Heat oil in large deep skillet over medium heat until hot. Add onion and bell pepper; cook and stir 1 minute. Add pasta, chicken, tomatoes, artichokes, olives and Italian seasoning; mix until blended.

4. Place half of chicken mixture in prepared dish; sprinkle with half of cheese. Top with remaining chicken mixture and cheese.

5. Bake, covered, 35 minutes or until hot and bubbly. *Makes 8 servings*

Artichoke-Olive Chicken Bake

Oriental Chicken & Rice

1 (6.9-ounce) package RICE-A-RONI® Chicken Flavor
2 tablespoons margarine or butter
1 pound boneless, skinless chicken breasts, cut into thin strips
¼ cup teriyaki sauce
½ teaspoon ground ginger
1 (16-ounce) package frozen Oriental-style mixed vegetables

1. In large skillet over medium heat, sauté rice-vermicelli mix with margarine until vermicelli is golden brown.

2. Slowly stir in 2 cups water, chicken, teriyaki sauce, ginger and Special Seasonings; bring to a boil. Reduce heat to low. Cover; simmer 10 minutes.

3. Stir in vegetables. Cover; simmer 5 to 10 minutes or until rice is tender and chicken is no longer pink inside. Let stand 3 minutes.   *Makes 4 servings*

Prep Time: 5 minutes
Cook Time: 25 minutes

Variation: Use pork instead of chicken and substitute ¼ cup orange juice for ¼ cup of the water.

Teriyaki is the term for a Japanese preparation of grilled meat or poultry that has first been marinated in a mixture of soy sauce, sake (Japanese rice wine), sugar and seasonings. The soy sauce and sugar combine to give the cooked food an appealing brown glaze. Teriyaki also can refer to a sauce made with these ingredients. It is sold bottled in most supermarkets and can be used for marinating or for adding flavor to simple stir-fry preparations.

Oriental Chicken & Rice

Chicken Enchilada Skillet Casserole

1 bag (16 ounces) BIRDS EYE® frozen Farm Fresh Mixtures Broccoli, Corn & Red Peppers
3 cups shredded cooked chicken
1 can (16 ounces) diced tomatoes, undrained
1 package (1¼ ounces) taco seasoning mix
1 cup shredded Monterey Jack cheese
8 ounces tortilla chips

• In large skillet, combine vegetables, chicken, tomatoes and seasoning mix; bring to boil over medium-high heat.

• Cover; cook 4 minutes or until vegetables are cooked and mixture is heated through.

• Sprinkle with cheese; cover and cook 2 minutes more or until cheese is melted.

• Serve with chips.   *Makes 4 servings*

Prep Time: 5 minutes
Cook Time: 10 minutes

Easy Asian Chicken Skillet

2 packages (3 ounces each) chicken flavor instant ramen noodles
1 package (10 ounces) frozen broccoli florets, thawed
1 package (9 ounces) frozen baby carrots, thawed
1 pound boneless skinless chicken breasts, cut into thin strips
1 tablespoon vegetable oil
1 can (8 ounces) sliced water chestnuts, drained
¼ cup stir-fry sauce

1. Remove seasoning packets from noodles. Save one packet for another use.

2. Bring 4 cups water to a boil in large saucepan. Add noodles, broccoli and carrots. Cook on medium-high heat 5 minutes, stirring occasionally; drain.

3. Heat oil in large nonstick skillet over medium-high heat. Add chicken; cook and stir until browned, about 8 minutes.

4. Stir in noodle mixture, water chestnuts, stir-fry sauce and one seasoning packet; cook until heated through.   *Makes 4 to 6 servings*

Chicken Enchilada Skillet Casserole

Heartland Chicken Casserole

10 slices white bread, cubed
1½ cups cracker or dry bread crumbs, divided
4 cups cubed cooked chicken
3 cups chicken broth
1 cup chopped onion
1 cup chopped celery
1 can (8 ounces) sliced mushrooms, drained
1 jar (about 4 ounces) pimientos, diced
3 eggs, lightly beaten
Salt and black pepper
1 tablespoon butter

1. Preheat oven to 350°F.

2. Combine bread cubes and 1 cup cracker crumbs in large mixing bowl. Add chicken, broth, onion, celery, mushrooms, pimientos and eggs; mix well. Season with salt and pepper; spoon into 2½-quart casserole.

3. Melt butter in small saucepan. Add remaining ½ cup cracker crumbs and brown, stirring occasionally. Sprinkle crumbs over casserole.

4. Bake 1 hour or until hot and bubbly.   *Makes 6 servings*

To make cracker crumbs quickly and neatly, place the whole crackers in a resealable plastic food storage bag. Seal the bag and then crush them with a rolling pin or a meat mallet.

Heartland Chicken Casserole

Creamy Chile and Chicken Casserole

3 tablespoons butter, divided
2 jalapeño peppers,* seeded and finely chopped
2 tablespoons all-purpose flour
½ cup heavy cream
1 cup chicken broth
1 cup (4 ounces) shredded sharp Cheddar cheese
1 cup (4 ounces) shredded Asiago cheese
1 stalk celery, chopped
1 cup sliced mushrooms
1 yellow squash, chopped
1 red bell pepper, chopped
12 ounces diced cooked chicken breast
¼ cup chopped green onions, including some green parts
¼ teaspoon salt
¼ teaspoon black pepper
½ cup sliced bacon-Cheddar flavored almonds

Jalapeño peppers can sting and irritate the skin, so wear rubber gloves when handling peppers and do not touch your eyes.

1. Preheat oven to 350°F. For cheese sauce, melt 2 tablespoons butter in medium saucepan. Add jalapeño peppers; cook and stir over high heat 1 minute. Add flour; stir to make paste. Add cream; stir until thickened. Add broth; stir until smooth. Gradually add cheeses, stirring to melt. Set aside.

2. Melt remaining 1 tablespoon butter in large skillet. Add celery, mushrooms, yellow squash and bell pepper. Cook and stir over high heat 3 to 5 minutes or until vegetables are tender. Remove from heat. Stir in chicken, green onions, salt and pepper. Stir in cheese sauce.

3. Spoon mixture into shallow 2-quart casserole dish. Sprinkle with almonds. Bake 10 minutes or until casserole is bubbly and hot.   *Makes 6 servings*

Creamy Chile and Chicken Casserole

Chicken & Broccoli with Garlic Sauce

    1 tablespoon BERTOLLI® Olive Oil
    4 boneless, skinless chicken breast halves (about 1¼ pounds)
    1 package (10 ounces) frozen broccoli florets, thawed
    1 envelope LIPTON® RECIPE SECRETS® Savory Herb with Garlic Soup
      Mix
  ¾ cup water
    1 teaspoon soy sauce

1. In 12-inch nonstick skillet, heat oil over medium-high heat and brown chicken. Remove chicken and set aside.

2. In same skillet, add broccoli and soup mix blended with water and soy sauce. Bring to a boil over high heat.

3. Return chicken to skillet. Reduce heat to low and simmer covered 10 minutes or until chicken is thoroughly cooked. Serve, if desired, over hot cooked rice.   *Makes 4 servings*

Easy Chicken Pot Pie

    2 cups cut-up cooked chicken
    1 package (10 ounces) frozen mixed vegetables, thawed
  1¼ cups milk
    1 envelope LIPTON® RECIPE SECRETS® Golden Onion Soup Mix*
    1 pie crust or pastry for single-crust pie

*Also terrific with LIPTON® RECIPE SECRETS® Savory Herb with Garlic Soup Mix.

1. Preheat oven to 400°F. In 9-inch pie plate, combine chicken and vegetables; set aside.

2. In small saucepan, bring milk and soup mix to a boil over medium heat, stirring occasionally. Cook 1 minute. Stir into chicken mixture.

3. Top with pie crust. Press pastry around edge of pie plate to seal; trim excess pastry, then flute edges. With tip of knife, make small slits in pastry.

4. Bake uncovered 35 minutes or until crust is golden.
                                              Makes about 4 servings

Serving Suggestion: Serve with your favorite LIPTON® Soup and LIPTON® Iced Tea.

Chicken & Broccoli with Garlic Sauce

Homestyle Skillet Chicken

  1 tablespoon Cajun seasoning blend
½ teaspoon plus ⅛ teaspoon black pepper, divided
½ teaspoon salt, divided
  4 chicken thighs
  2 tablespoons vegetable oil
  4 cloves garlic, minced
¾ pound small red or new potatoes (about 8), quartered
12 pearl onions, peeled*
  1 cup baby carrots
  2 stalks celery, halved lengthwise and sliced diagonally into ½-inch pieces
½ red bell pepper, diced
  2 tablespoons all-purpose flour
  1 cup reduced-sodium chicken broth
½ cup sherry
  2 tablespoons finely chopped fresh parsley

To peel pearl onions, drop into boiling water for 30 seconds, then plunge immediately into ice water. The peel should slide right off.

1. Combine Cajun seasoning, ½ teaspoon black pepper and ¼ teaspoon salt in small bowl. Rub mixture onto all sides of chicken.

2. Heat oil in large heavy skillet over medium-high heat. Add garlic and chicken; cook until chicken is browned, about 3 minutes per side. Transfer chicken to plate; set aside.

3. Add potatoes, onions, carrots, celery and bell pepper to skillet. Cook and stir 3 minutes. Sprinkle flour over vegetables; stir to coat. Slowly stir in chicken broth and sherry, scraping up browned bits from bottom of skillet. Bring mixture to a boil, stirring constantly.

4. Reduce heat to medium-low. Return chicken to skillet. Cover and cook about 30 minutes or until juices of chicken run clear. Increase heat to medium-high; cook, uncovered, about 5 minutes or until sauce is thickened.

5. Season with remaining ¼ teaspoon salt and ⅛ teaspoon black pepper. Sprinkle with parsley just before serving.   *Makes 4 servings*

Homestyle Skillet Chicken

Almond Chicken

1½ cups water
4 tablespoons dry sherry, divided
4½ teaspoons plus 1 tablespoon cornstarch, divided
4 teaspoons soy sauce
1 teaspoon instant chicken bouillon granules
1 egg white
½ teaspoon salt
4 whole boneless skinless chicken breasts, cut into 1-inch pieces
Vegetable oil for frying
½ cup blanched whole almonds (about 3 ounces)
1 large carrot, diced
1 teaspoon minced fresh ginger
6 green onions, cut into 1-inch pieces
3 stalks celery, diagonally cut into ½-inch pieces
8 fresh mushrooms, sliced
½ cup sliced bamboo shoots (½ of 8-ounce can), drained

1. Combine water, 2 tablespoons sherry, 4½ teaspoons cornstarch, soy sauce and bouillon granules in small saucepan. Cook and stir over medium heat until mixture boils and thickens, about 5 minutes. Keep warm.

2. Combine remaining 2 tablespoons sherry, 1 tablespoon cornstarch, egg white and salt in medium bowl. Add chicken pieces; stir to coat well.

3. Heat oil in wok or large skillet over high heat to 375°F. Add half the chicken pieces, one at a time; cook 3 to 5 minutes until light brown. Drain on paper towels. Repeat with remaining chicken.

4. Remove all but 2 tablespoons oil from wok. Add almonds; stir-fry until golden, about 2 minutes. Transfer almonds to small bowl; set aside. Add carrot and ginger to wok; stir-fry 1 minute. Add green onions, celery, mushrooms and bamboo shoots; stir-fry until crisp-tender, about 3 minutes. Stir in chicken, almonds and sauce; cook and stir until heated through.

Makes 4 to 6 servings

Almond Chicken

Dairyland Confetti Chicken

 1 cup diced carrots
 ¾ cup chopped onion
 ½ cup diced celery
 ¼ cup chicken broth
 3 cups cubed cooked chicken
 1 can (10½ ounces) cream of chicken soup, undiluted
 1 cup dairy sour cream
 ½ cup (4 ounces) sliced mushrooms
 1 teaspoon Worcestershire sauce
 1 teaspoon salt
 ⅛ teaspoon black pepper
   Confetti Topping (recipe follows)
 ¼ cup (1 ounce) shredded Wisconsin Cheddar cheese

For casserole, in saucepan, combine carrots, onion, celery and chicken broth. Simmer 20 minutes. In 3-quart casserole, mix cubed chicken, soup, sour cream, mushrooms, Worcestershire sauce, salt and pepper. Add simmered vegetables and liquid; mix well. Prepare Confetti Topping. Drop tablespoons of Confetti Topping onto casserole. Bake in 350°F oven for 40 to 45 minutes or until golden brown. Sprinkle with cheese and return to oven until melted. Garnish as desired.   *Makes 6 to 8 servings*

Confetti Topping

 1 cup sifted all-purpose flour
 2 teaspoons baking powder
 ½ teaspoon salt
 2 eggs, lightly beaten
 ½ cup milk
 1 tablespoon chopped green bell pepper
 1 tablespoon chopped pimiento
 1 cup (4 ounces) shredded Wisconsin Cheddar cheese

In mixing bowl, combine flour, baking powder and salt. Add eggs, milk, green pepper, pimiento and cheese. Mix just until well blended.

Favorite recipe from **Wisconsin Milk Marketing Board**

Dairyland Confetti Chicken

Chicken Florentine in Minutes

3 cups water
1 cup milk
2 tablespoons butter
2 packages (about 4 ounces each) fettuccine Alfredo or stroganoff pasta mix
4 cups fresh baby spinach, coarsely chopped
¼ teaspoon black pepper
1 package (about 10 ounces) refrigerated fully cooked chicken breast strips, cut in bite-size pieces
¼ cup diced roasted red peppers
¼ cup sour cream

1. Bring water, milk and butter to a boil in large saucepan over medium-high heat. Stir in pasta mixes, spinach and black pepper. Reduce heat to medium. Cook 8 minutes or until pasta is tender, stirring occasionally.

2. Stir in chicken and red peppers. Cook 2 minutes or until hot. Remove from heat. Stir in sour cream.   *Makes 4 servings*

Chicken Casserole Olé

12 boneless skinless chicken tenders
2 cups water
1 can (15 ounces) mild chili beans, undrained
1 cup salsa
½ cup chopped green bell pepper
2 cups UNCLE BEN'S® Instant Rice
2 cups (8 ounces) shredded Mexican cheese blend, divided
2 cups bite-size tortilla chips

1. Spray large skillet with nonstick cooking spray. Add chicken; cook over medium-high heat 12 to 15 minutes or until lightly browned on both sides and chicken is no longer pink in center.

2. Add water, beans with liquid, salsa and bell pepper. Bring to a boil; add rice and 1 cup cheese. Cover; remove from heat and let stand 5 minutes or until liquid is absorbed. Top with tortilla chips and remaining 1 cup cheese; let stand, covered, 3 to 5 minutes or until cheese is melted.

Makes 6 servings

Chicken Florentine in Minutes

Coq au Vin & Pasta

4 large or 8 small chicken thighs (2 to 2½ pounds), trimmed of excess fat
2 teaspoons rotisserie or herb chicken seasoning*
1 tablespoon margarine or butter
3 cups (8 ounces) halved or quartered mushrooms
1 medium onion, coarsely chopped
½ cup dry white wine or vermouth
1 (4.9-ounce) package PASTA RONI® Homestyle Chicken Flavor
½ cup sliced green onions

1 teaspoon paprika and 1 teaspoon garlic salt can be substituted.

1. Sprinkle meaty side of chicken with rotisserie seasoning. In large skillet over medium-high heat, melt margarine. Add chicken, seasoned-side down; cook 3 minutes. Reduce heat to medium-low; turn chicken over.

2. Add mushrooms, onion and wine. Cover; simmer 15 to 18 minutes or until chicken is no longer pink inside. Remove chicken from skillet; set aside.

3. In same skillet, bring 1 cup water to a boil. Stir in pasta, green onions and Special Seasonings. Place chicken over pasta. Reduce heat to medium-low. Cover; gently boil 6 to 8 minutes or until pasta is tender. Let stand 3 to 5 minutes before serving.
Makes 4 servings

Prep Time: 10 minutes
Cook Time: 30 minutes

Wines of all sorts are used in cooking. Special cooking wines available in supermarkets are not recommended because they are often inferior in quality and contain salt. However, there is no need to use fine vintages for cooking. It is not economical. Leftover wine that is no longer good for drinking can be used in cooking.

Coq au Vin & Pasta

Bistro in a Pot

2 tablespoons Lucini Premium Select extra virgin olive oil
½ to 1 pound boneless skinless chicken, cut into bite-size pieces
½ cup minced shallots
2 large cloves garlic, sliced
2 cups chopped leeks, white and light green parts, washed and drained
1½ cups baby carrots, cut into quarters lengthwise
1 cup thinly sliced new potatoes
3 to 4 teaspoons dried lemon peel
2 tablespoons dried tarragon leaves
½ cup water
1 cup shredded JARLSBERG LITE™ cheese
1 cup frozen peas, thawed (optional)
Minced fresh parsley for garnish

In wok or large skillet with cover, heat olive oil over high heat until nearly smoking. Stir-fry chicken, shallots and garlic. Remove to bowl. Add leeks to wok and stir-fry 3 minutes. Add to chicken mixture. Add carrots, potatoes, lemon peel and tarragon to wok; stir-fry 5 minutes. Return chicken mixture to wok. Add ½ cup water; stir quickly. Cover tightly and steam 5 minutes. (Add more water if necessary.)

Remove from heat; add cheese and peas, if desired. Stir and serve.

Makes 4 to 6 servings

Serving Suggestion: Serve with a green salad and light sourdough French bread or crusty rolls.

Spinach Chicken Manicotti

  8 uncooked manicotti shells
¼ teaspoon salt
½ teaspoon black pepper, divided
12 ounces boneless skinless chicken breasts
  1 package (10 ounces) frozen chopped spinach, thawed and squeezed dry
  1 container (16 ounces) cottage cheese
½ cup (2 ounces) crumbled blue cheese
  4 cloves garlic, minced
  1 can (14½ ounces) spaghetti sauce, divided

1. Cook pasta according to package directions, omitting salt. Drain; set aside.

2. Meanwhile, fill medium saucepan with water. Add salt and ¼ teaspoon pepper. Bring to a boil over high heat; add chicken. Reduce heat to medium; simmer, covered, about 30 minutes or until chicken is tender and no longer pink in center. Remove chicken from saucepan. Let cool slightly; shred.

3. Preheat oven to 350°F. Spray 11×7-inch baking pan with nonstick cooking spray; set aside. Combine spinach, cottage cheese, blue cheese, garlic, remaining ¼ teaspoon pepper and chicken in large bowl. Pour half the spaghetti sauce into bottom of prepared pan. Fill manicotti with chicken mixture. Place in sauce in pan; top with remaining spaghetti sauce. Bake, covered, 20 minutes or until heated through. *Makes 4 servings*

*To easily fill the manicotti shells, spoon the chicken
mixture into a 1-quart food storage bag. Cut a small hole in one
corner and then simply pipe the mixture into the shells.*

Country Chicken Stew with Dumplings

1 tablespoon BERTOLLI® Olive Oil
1 chicken (3 to 3½ pounds), cut into serving pieces (with or without skin)
4 large carrots, cut into 2-inch pieces
3 ribs celery, cut into 1-inch pieces
1 large onion, cut into 1-inch wedges
1 envelope LIPTON® RECIPE SECRETS® Savory Herb with Garlic Soup Mix*
1½ cups water
½ cup apple juice
Parsley Dumplings (optional, recipe follows)

Also terrific with LIPTON® RECIPE SECRETS® Golden Onion Soup Mix.

1. In 6-quart Dutch oven or heavy saucepot, heat oil over medium-high heat and brown half of the chicken; remove and set aside. Repeat with remaining chicken. Return chicken to Dutch oven. Stir in carrots, celery, onion and soup mix blended with water and apple juice. Bring to a boil over high heat. Reduce heat to low; simmer, covered, 25 minutes or until chicken is thoroughly cooked, juices run clear and vegetables are tender.

2. Meanwhile, prepare Parsley Dumplings. Drop 12 rounded tablespoonfuls of batter into simmering broth around chicken. Continue simmering, covered, 10 minutes or until toothpick inserted into center of dumplings comes out clean. Season stew, if desired, with salt and pepper.   *Makes about 6 servings*

Parsley Dumplings: In medium bowl, combine 1⅓ cups all-purpose flour, 2 teaspoons baking powder, 1 tablespoon chopped fresh parsley and ½ teaspoon salt; set aside. In measuring cup, blend ⅔ cup milk, 2 tablespoons melted butter or margarine and 1 egg. Stir milk mixture into flour mixture just until blended.

Variation: Add 1 pound quartered red potatoes to stew with carrots; omit dumplings.

Country Chicken Stew with Dumplings

Chicken Tetrazzini with Roasted Red Peppers

6 ounces uncooked egg noodles
3 tablespoons butter or margarine
¼ cup all-purpose flour
1 can (about 14 ounces) chicken broth
1 cup whipping cream
2 tablespoons dry sherry
2 cans (6 ounces each) sliced mushrooms, drained
1 jar (about 7 ounces) roasted red peppers, drained and cut into ½-inch strips
2 cups chopped cooked chicken
1 teaspoon Italian seasoning
½ cup (2 ounces) grated Parmesan cheese

1. Cook egg noodles according to package directions. Drain well.

2. Meanwhile, melt butter in medium saucepan over medium heat. Add flour and whisk until smooth. Add chicken broth; bring to a boil over high heat. Remove from heat. Gradually add whipping cream and sherry; stir until well blended.

3. Combine mushrooms, red peppers and noodles in large bowl; toss well. Add half the chicken broth mixture to noodle mixture; stir. Combine remaining chicken broth mixture, chicken and Italian seasoning in large bowl.

4. Spoon noodle mixture into serving dish. Make a well in center of noodles; spoon chicken mixture into well. Sprinkle with cheese. *Makes 6 servings*

Prep and Cook Time: 20 minutes

Chicken Tetrazzini with Roasted Red Peppers

Chicken Pot Pie with Onion Biscuits

     1 package (1.8 ounces) classic white sauce mix
2¾ cups milk, divided
     ¼ teaspoon dried thyme leaves
     1 package (10 ounces) frozen peas and carrots, thawed
     1 package (10 ounces) roasted carved chicken breast, cut into bite-size
          pieces
     1 cup all-purpose baking mix
1⅓ cups *French's*® French Fried Onions, divided
     ½ cup (2 ounces) shredded Cheddar cheese

1. Preheat oven to 400°F. Prepare white sauce mix according to package directions with 2¼ cups milk; stir in thyme. Mix vegetables, chicken and prepared white sauce in shallow 2-quart casserole.

2. Combine baking mix, ⅔ *cup* French Fried Onions and remaining ½ cup milk in medium bowl until blended. Drop 6 to 8 spoonfuls of dough over chicken mixture.

3. Bake 25 minutes or until biscuits are golden. Sprinkle biscuits with cheese and remaining ⅔ *cup* onions. Bake 3 minutes or until cheese is melted and onions are golden.   *Makes 6 servings*

Prep Time: 15 minutes
Cook Time: 28 minutes

Tip: You can substitute 2 cups cut-up cooked chicken for the roasted, carved chicken breast.

Variation: For added Cheddar flavor, substitute *French's*® **Cheddar French Fried Onions** for the original flavor.

Spicy Chicken Casserole with Corn Bread

2 tablespoons olive oil
4 boneless skinless chicken breasts, cut into bite-size pieces
1 envelope (about 1 ounce) taco seasoning
1 can (about 15 ounces) black beans, rinsed and drained
1 can (14½ ounces) diced tomatoes, drained
1 can (about 10 ounces) Mexican-style corn, drained
1 can (about 4 ounces) diced green chiles, drained
½ cup mild salsa
1 box (about 8½ ounces) corn bread mix, plus ingredients to prepare mix
½ cup (2 ounces) shredded Cheddar cheese
¼ cup chopped red bell pepper

1. Preheat oven to 350°F. Spray 2-quart casserole with nonstick cooking spray. Set aside. Heat oil in large skillet over medium heat. Cook chicken until cooked through.

2. Sprinkle taco seasoning over chicken. Add black beans, tomatoes, corn, chiles and salsa; stir until well blended. Transfer to prepared dish.

3. Prepare corn bread mix according to package directions, adding cheese and bell pepper. Spread batter over chicken mixture.

4. Bake 30 minutes or until corn bread is golden brown.

Makes 4 to 6 servings

Spicy Chicken Casserole with Corn Bread

Chicken, Asparagus & Mushroom Bake

1 tablespoon butter
1 tablespoon olive oil
2 boneless skinless chicken breasts (about ½ pound), cut into bite-size pieces
2 cloves garlic, minced
1 cup sliced mushrooms
2 cups sliced asparagus
   Black pepper
1 package (about 6 ounces) corn bread stuffing mix
¼ cup dry white wine (optional)
1 can (about 14 ounces) reduced-sodium chicken broth
1 can (about 10 ounces) condensed cream of asparagus or cream of chicken soup, undiluted

1. Preheat oven to 350°F. Heat butter and oil in large skillet until butter is melted. Cook and stir chicken and garlic about 3 minutes over medium-high heat until chicken is no longer pink. Add mushrooms; cook and stir 2 minutes. Add asparagus; cook and stir about 5 minutes or until asparagus is crisp-tender. Season with pepper.

2. Transfer mixture to 2½-quart casserole or 6 small casseroles. Top with stuffing mix.

3. Add wine to skillet, if desired; cook and stir 1 minute over medium-high heat, scraping up any browned bits from bottom of skillet. Add broth and soup; cook and stir until well blended.

4. Pour broth mixture into casserole; mix well. Bake, uncovered, about 35 minutes (30 minutes for small casseroles) or until heated through and lightly browned.

Makes 6 servings

Chicken, Asparagus & Mushroom Bake

Sweet & Sour Chicken and Rice

1 pound chicken tenders
1 can (8 ounces) pineapple chunks, drained and juice reserved
1 cup uncooked rice
2 carrots, thinly sliced
1 green bell pepper, cut into 1-inch pieces
1 large onion, chopped
3 cloves garlic, minced
1 can (about 14 ounces) reduced-sodium chicken broth
⅓ cup soy sauce
3 tablespoons sugar
3 tablespoons apple cider vinegar
1 tablespoon sesame oil
1½ teaspoons ground ginger
¼ cup chopped peanuts (optional)
Chopped fresh cilantro (optional)

1. Preheat oven to 350°F. Spray 13×9-inch baking dish with nonstick cooking spray.

2. Combine chicken, pineapple, rice, carrots, bell pepper, onion and garlic in prepared dish.

3. Place broth, reserved pineapple juice, soy sauce, sugar, vinegar, sesame oil and ginger in small saucepan; bring to a boil over high heat. Remove from heat and pour over chicken mixture.

4. Cover tightly with foil; bake 40 to 50 minutes or until chicken is no longer pink in centers and rice is tender. Sprinkle with peanuts and cilantro, if desired.

Makes 6 servings

Sweet & Sour Chicken and Rice

Savory Chicken and Biscuits

1 pound boneless, skinless chicken thighs or breasts, cut into 1-inch pieces
1 medium potato, cut into 1-inch pieces
1 medium yellow onion, cut into 1-inch pieces
8 ounces fresh mushrooms, quartered
1 cup fresh baby carrots
1 cup chopped celery
1 (14½-ounce) can chicken broth
3 cloves garlic, minced
1 teaspoon dried rosemary leaves
1 teaspoon salt
1 teaspoon black pepper
3 tablespoons cornstarch blended with ½ cup cold water
1 cup frozen peas, thawed
1 (4-ounce) jar sliced pimientos, drained
1 package BOB EVANS® Frozen Buttermilk Biscuit Dough

Preheat oven to 375°F. Combine chicken, potato, onion, mushrooms, carrots, celery, broth, garlic, rosemary, salt and pepper in large saucepan. Bring to a boil over high heat. Reduce heat to low and simmer, uncovered, 5 minutes. Stir in cornstarch mixture; cook 2 minutes. Stir in peas and pimientos; return to a boil. Transfer chicken mixture to 2-quart casserole dish; arrange frozen biscuits on top. Bake 30 to 35 minutes or until biscuits are golden brown. Refrigerate leftovers.

Makes 4 to 6 servings

Savory Chicken and Biscuits

Chicken & White Bean Stew

1 tablespoon olive oil

2 medium carrots, sliced (about 2 cups)

1 medium onion, thinly sliced

2 cloves garlic, finely chopped

1 tablespoon balsamic vinegar

1 pound boneless, skinless chicken breast halves or thighs, cut into chunks

1 jar (1 pound 10 ounces) RAGÚ® Old World Style® Pasta Sauce

2 cans (15 ounces each) cannellini or white kidney beans, rinsed and drained

Pinch crushed red pepper flakes (optional)

1. In 12-inch skillet, heat olive oil over medium heat and cook carrots, onion and garlic, stirring occasionally, 5 minutes or until vegetables are tender. Stir in vinegar and cook 1 minute. Remove vegetables; set aside.

2. In same skillet, thoroughly brown chicken over medium-high heat. Return vegetables to skillet. Stir in Ragú Old World Style Pasta Sauce, beans and red pepper flakes. Bring to a boil over high heat. Reduce heat to medium and simmer covered, stirring occasionally, 15 minutes or until chicken is thoroughly cooked. Garnish, if desired, with fresh parsley and serve with toasted Italian bread.
Makes 6 servings

Balsamic vinegar is an Italian aged vinegar with a distinctive mellow flavor. Its dark brown color is derived from the wood barrels in which it is aged. Look for it in the imported section of the supermarket or in specialty food shops.

Chicken & White Bean Stew

Orange Chicken Stir-Fry

½ cup orange juice

2 tablespoons sesame oil, divided

2 tablespoons soy sauce

1 tablespoon dry sherry

2 teaspoons freshly grated fresh ginger

1 teaspoon freshly grated orange peel

1 clove garlic, minced

1½ pounds boneless skinless chicken breasts, cut into strips

3 cups mixed fresh vegetables, such as green bell pepper, red bell pepper, snow peas, carrots, green onions, mushrooms and/or onions

1 tablespoon cornstarch

½ cup unsalted cashew bits or halves

3 cups hot cooked rice

Combine orange juice, 1 tablespoon oil, soy sauce, sherry, ginger, orange peel and garlic in large glass bowl. Add chicken; marinate in refrigerator 1 hour. Drain chicken, reserving marinade. Heat remaining 1 tablespoon oil in large skillet or wok over medium-high heat. Add chicken; stir-fry 3 minutes or until chicken is light brown. Add vegetables; stir-fry 3 to 5 minutes or until vegetables are crisp-tender. Combine cornstarch and marinade; add to skillet and stir until sauce boils and thickens. Stir in cashews; cook 1 minute more. Serve over hot rice. *Makes 6 servings*

Favorite recipe from **USA Rice**

Dried, ground ginger tastes very different from fresh, so the two types are not interchangeable in recipes. Resembling a gnarled, tan-colored root, fresh ginger adds its own distinctive pungency and aroma to foods. Buy fresh ginger (also called gingerroot) in small quantities and store it, unpeeled, tightly wrapped in the refrigerator for two weeks. For freshly grated ginger, first peel away the rough outer skin, then grate the flesh on a ginger grater (sold in many Asian markets) or other fine grater.

Orange Chicken Stir-Fry

Chicken & Wild Rice with Indian Flavors

¾ teaspoon salt
¾ teaspoon ground cumin
½ teaspoon black pepper
½ teaspoon ground cinnamon
½ teaspoon ground turmeric
4 boneless skinless chicken breast halves (about 1½ pounds)
1¼ cups chicken broth
1 cup water
¾ cup wild rice
2 tablespoons olive oil, divided
1 onion, chopped
2 carrots sliced
1 red bell pepper, chopped
1 stalk celery, chopped
2 cloves garlic, minced
¼ cup sliced almonds

1. Combine salt, cumin, black pepper, cinnamon and turmeric in small bowl. Rub spice mixture on both sides of chicken breasts. Place chicken on plate; cover and refrigerate at least 30 minutes or up to 3 hours.

2. Meanwhile, bring chicken broth and water to a boil in large saucepan. Stir in wild rice. Cover; reduce heat to low. Cook about 45 minutes or until rice is almost tender.

3. When rice is almost done, preheat oven to 350°F. Coat 13×9-inch baking dish with nonstick cooking spray. Heat 1 tablespoon oil in large skillet over medium heat. Add chicken and brown on both sides; set aside.

4. Add remaining 1 tablespoon oil to same skillet. Cook and stir onion, carrots, bell pepper, celery and garlic 5 to 10 minutes or until crisp-tender.

5. Stir vegetables into cooked rice in saucepan. Spread rice-vegetable mixture in prepared baking dish. Top with chicken breasts; sprinkle with almonds. Cover tightly with foil; bake 30 minutes or until chicken is no longer pink in center and rice is tender.
Makes 4 servings

Chicken & Wild Rice with Indian Flavors

Chicken Bourguignonne

4 pounds boneless skinless chicken thighs and breasts
   All-purpose flour
2 cups reduced-sodium chicken broth
2 cups dry white wine or additional chicken broth
1 pound whole baby carrots
¼ cup tomato paste
4 cloves garlic, minced
½ teaspoon dried thyme
2 bay leaves
¼ teaspoon salt
¼ teaspoon black pepper
8 ounces fresh or thawed frozen pearl onions
8 ounces whole medium mushrooms
2 cups hot cooked white rice
2 cups hot cooked wild rice
¼ cup minced fresh parsley

1. Preheat oven to 325°F. Coat chicken very lightly with flour. Generously spray nonstick ovenproof Dutch oven or large nonstick ovenproof skillet with cooking spray; heat over medium heat until hot. Cook chicken 10 to 15 minutes or until browned on all sides. Drain fat from Dutch oven.

2. Add chicken broth, wine, carrots, tomato paste, garlic, thyme, bay leaves, salt and pepper to Dutch oven; heat to a boil. Cover; transfer to oven. Bake 1 hour. Add onions and mushrooms. Uncover; bake about 35 minutes or until vegetables are tender, and chicken is no longer pink in center and juices run clear. Remove and discard bay leaves. Combine white and wild rice; serve with chicken. Sprinkle with parsley. *Makes 8 servings*

Chicken Bourguignonne

Broccoli, Turkey and Noodle Skillet

1 tablespoon butter
1 green bell pepper, chopped
1 cup frozen chopped broccoli, thawed
¼ teaspoon black pepper
1½ cups chicken broth
½ cup milk or half-and-half
2 cups diced cooked turkey breast
1 package (about 4 ounces) chicken and
    broccoli pasta mix
¼ cup sour cream

1. Melt butter in large nonstick skillet over medium-high heat. Add bell pepper, broccoli and black pepper. Cook 5 minutes or until bell pepper is crisp-tender. Add chicken broth and milk. Bring to a boil. Stir in turkey and pasta mix.

2. Reduce heat to low. Cook 8 to 10 minutes or until noodles are tender. Stir in sour cream. Remove from heat. Let stand, uncovered, 5 minutes or until sauce is thickened.

Makes 4 servings

Broccoli, Turkey and Noodle Skillet

Turkey-Olive Ragoût en Crust

½ pound boneless white or dark turkey meat, cut into 1-inch cubes
1 clove garlic, minced
1 teaspoon vegetable oil
¼ cup (about 10) small whole frozen onions
½ cup reduced-sodium chicken broth or turkey broth
½ teaspoon dried parsley flakes
⅛ teaspoon dried thyme leaves
1 small bay leaf
1 medium red potato, skin on, cut into ½-inch cubes
10 frozen snow peas
8 whole small pitted ripe olives
1 can (4 ounces) refrigerated crescent rolls
½ teaspoon dried dill weed

1. Preheat oven to 375°F.

2. In medium skillet over medium heat, cook and stir turkey in garlic and oil 3 to 4 minutes or until no longer pink; remove and set aside. Add onions to skillet; cook and stir until lightly browned. Add broth, parsley, thyme, bay leaf and potato. Bring mixture to a boil. Reduce heat; cover and simmer 10 minutes or until potato is tender. Remove and discard bay leaf.

3. Combine turkey mixture with potato mixture. Stir in snow peas and olives. Divide hot mixture between 2 (1¾-cup) individual ovenproof casseroles.

4. Divide crescent rolls into 2 rectangles; press perforations together to seal. If necessary, roll out each rectangle to make dough large enough to cover top of each casserole. Sprinkle dough with dill weed, pressing lightly into dough. Cut small decorative shape from each dough piece. Place dough over turkey-vegetable mixture in casseroles. Trim dough to fit; press dough to edge of each casserole to seal. Bake 8 to 15 minutes or until pastry is golden brown.

Makes 2 individual deep-dish pies

Lattice Crust Variation: With pastry wheel or knife, cut each rectangle lengthwise into 6 strips. Arrange strips, lattice-fashion, over turkey-vegetable mixture; trim dough to fit. Press ends of dough to edge of each casserole to seal.

Note: For more golden crust, brush top of dough with beaten egg yolk before baking.

*Favorite recipe from **National Turkey Federation***

Turkey-Olive Ragoût en Crust

Spicy Turkey Casserole

1 tablespoon olive oil
1 pound turkey breast cutlets, cut into ½-inch pieces
2 spicy turkey sausages (about 3 ounces each), sliced ½ inch thick
1 cup diced green bell pepper
½ cup sliced mushrooms
½ cup diced onion
1 jalapeño pepper,* seeded and minced (optional)
½ cup reduced-sodium chicken broth or water
1 can (about 14 ounces) diced tomatoes, undrained
1 teaspoon Italian seasoning
¼ teaspoon black pepper
½ teaspoon paprika
1 cup cooked egg noodles
6 tablespoons grated Parmesan cheese
2 tablespoons coarse bread crumbs

Jalapeño peppers can sting and irritate the skin, so wear rubber gloves when handling peppers and do not touch your eyes.

1. Preheat oven to 350°F. Heat oil in large nonstick skillet. Add turkey and sausages; cook and stir over medium heat 2 minutes. Add bell pepper, mushrooms, onion and jalapeño pepper, if desired; cook and stir 5 minutes. Add chicken broth; cook 1 minute, scraping up any browned bits from bottom of skillet. Add tomatoes with juice, seasonings and noodles.

2. Spoon turkey mixture into shallow 10-inch round casserole. Sprinkle with cheese and bread crumbs. Bake 15 to 20 minutes or until mixture is hot and bread crumbs are brown. Garnish as desired.   *Makes 6 (1-cup) servings*

Pasta should be cooked at a fast boil. This method circulates the pasta during cooking so that the cooking results will be more consistent. Always check the package for the manufacturer's recommended cooking time. Pasta that is to be baked in a casserole should be slightly undercooked or it will be too soft after baking.

Spicy Turkey Casserole

Triathlete's Turkey Chili

2 tablespoons vegetable oil
2 medium onions, finely chopped
2 small red or green bell peppers, finely chopped
2 pounds ground turkey
2 cans (about 14 ounces each) diced tomatoes
1 can (about 14 ounces) beef broth
1 cup water
¼ cup tomato paste
2 teaspoons chili powder
   Salt and black pepper to taste
1 can (15 ounces) kidney beans, rinsed and drained
1 can (15 ounces) pinto beans, rinsed and drained
   Cooked rice or corn bread (optional)
   Sour cream, shredded Cheddar cheese and green onion slices (optional)

1. Heat oil in Dutch oven. Add onions and bell peppers; cook and stir 3 minutes over medium heat. Add turkey; cook 3 minutes, stirring to break up meat. Stir in tomatoes, broth, water, tomato paste, chili powder, salt and pepper. Bring to a boil. Reduce heat and simmer 30 minutes, stirring often. If chili is too thick, add water, ½ cup at a time, until desired consistency is reached.

2. Add beans and cook 10 minutes or until beans are hot. Serve with rice or corn bread. Garnish with sour cream, cheese and green onion.

Makes 8 servings

Prep Time: 30 minutes
Cook Time: 46 minutes

Triathlete's Turkey Chili

Spinach & Turkey Skillet

  6 ounces turkey breast tenderloin
⅛ teaspoon salt
  2 teaspoons olive oil
¼ cup chopped onion
  2 cloves garlic, minced
⅓ cup uncooked rice
¾ teaspoon dried Italian seasoning
¼ teaspoon black pepper
  1 cup reduced-sodium chicken broth, divided
  2 cups torn fresh spinach leaves
⅔ cup diced plum tomatoes
  3 tablespoons freshly grated Parmesan cheese

1. Cut turkey tenderloin into bite-size pieces; sprinkle with salt.

2. Heat oil in medium skillet over medium-high heat. Add turkey pieces; cook and stir until lightly browned. Remove from skillet. Reduce heat to low. Add onion and garlic; cook and stir until tender. Return turkey to skillet. Stir in rice, Italian seasoning and pepper.

3. Reserve 2 tablespoons chicken broth. Stir remaining broth into mixture in skillet. Bring to a boil. Reduce heat; simmer, covered, 14 minutes. Stir in spinach and reserved broth. Cover; cook 2 to 3 minutes or until liquid is absorbed and spinach is wilted. Stir in tomatoes; heat through. Sprinkle with Parmesan cheese. *Makes 2 servings*

*Turkey breasts, sold whole or as halves, are available with the
bone in, boned and rolled, as boneless halves and as breast
cutlets. Store fresh turkey in the coldest part of the refrigerator
and use within two days of the "last sale date."*

Spinach & Turkey Skillet

Cha-Cha-Cha Casserole

   Nonstick cooking spray
1 can (about 7 ounces) whole green chiles, drained
1 pound ground turkey
1 cup chopped onion
1 tablespoon chili powder or to taste
3 cloves garlic, minced
1 teaspoon ground cumin
1 teaspoon salt (optional)
1 can (10 ounces) diced tomatoes with green chiles, undrained
2 cups frozen corn, thawed or canned corn, drained
1 can (16 ounces) refried beans
2 cups (8 ounces) shredded Mexican cheese blend
2 cups crushed tortilla chips
1 cup diced seeded fresh tomato
½ cup sliced green onions

1. Preheat oven to 375°F. Spray 8-inch square baking dish with cooking spray. Cut chiles in half lengthwise; place in single layer in prepared dish.

2. Spray medium nonstick skillet with cooking spray. Cook and stir turkey, onion, chili powder, garlic, cumin and salt, if desired, over medium heat until turkey is no longer pink. Add canned tomatoes with juice; cook about 10 minutes or until liquid evaporates.

3. Spoon turkey mixture over chiles; top with corn and beans. Sprinkle with cheese and crushed chips. Bake 30 minutes; let stand 5 minutes before serving. Garnish with fresh tomato and green onions.   *Makes 6 servings*

Cha-Cha-Cha Casserole

Saucy-Spicy Turkey Meatballs

1 pound ground turkey
⅓ cup dry bread crumbs
1 egg
1 clove garlic, minced
2 tablespoons light soy sauce, divided
1 teaspoon grated fresh ginger
¾ to 1 teaspoon red pepper flakes, divided
1 tablespoon vegetable oil
1 can (20 ounces) pineapple chunks, undrained
2 tablespoons lemon juice or orange juice
2 tablespoons honey
1 tablespoon cornstarch
1 large red bell pepper, seeded and cut into 1-inch triangles
Hot cooked rice

1. Combine turkey, bread crumbs, egg, garlic, 1 tablespoon soy sauce, ginger and ½ teaspoon red pepper flakes in large bowl. Shape into 1-inch meatballs.

2. Heat oil in wok or large skillet over medium-high heat. Add meatballs and cook 4 to 5 minutes or until no longer pink in centers, turning to brown all sides. Remove from wok; set aside.

3. Drain pineapple chunks, reserving juice. Add enough water to juice to make 1 cup. Whisk together pineapple juice mixture, lemon juice, honey, cornstarch, remaining 1 tablespoon soy sauce and ¼ teaspoon red pepper flakes. Pour into wok. Cook and stir over medium-high heat until sauce thickens.

4. Add meatballs, pineapple chunks and bell pepper to sauce. Cook and stir until hot. Adjust seasoning with remaining ¼ teaspoon hot pepper flakes, if desired. Serve over rice. *Makes 4 to 5 servings*

Turkey Stuffed Pasta Italiano

1 pound ground California turkey
1 cup minced onion
1 cup grated peeled eggplant
2 cloves garlic, minced
  Salt and black pepper
1 can (28 ounces) tomatoes, undrained
1 can (8 ounces) tomato sauce
1 cup red wine or water
1 teaspoon garlic salt
1 teaspoon dried oregano leaves
1 teaspoon dried basil leaves
½ teaspoon dried tarragon leaves
½ teaspoon crushed red pepper
1 package (12 ounces) uncooked jumbo pasta shells
½ cup grated Parmesan cheese
¾ cup (3 ounces) shredded mozzarella cheese

In large nonstick skillet, brown turkey, onion, eggplant and garlic until turkey is no longer pink; drain. Season with salt and black pepper; set aside. In small saucepan, simmer tomatoes with juice, tomato sauce, wine and seasonings for 15 minutes. Meanwhile, cook pasta shells until done, but still firm; drain. In large bowl, combine turkey mixture, Parmesan cheese and half the tomato sauce mixture. Stuff shells; place in 13×9-inch pan. Spoon remaining sauce mixture over shells; top with mozzarella cheese. Bake at 350°F for 30 minutes.

Makes 8 to 10 servings

Note: Shells can be stuffed ahead of time and refrigerated. Add sauce and mozzarella cheese just before baking. Increase cooking time by 8 to 10 minutes.

*Favorite recipe from **California Poultry Federation***

Skillet Turkey Tetrazzini

 2 tablespoons margarine or butter
¾ pound boneless, skinless turkey breast or chicken breasts, cut into thin
    strips
 1 cup sliced fresh mushrooms
½ cup chopped red or green bell pepper
⅔ cup milk
 1 (5.1-ounce) package PASTA RONI® Angel Hair Pasta with Parmesan
    Cheese

1. In large skillet over medium-high heat, melt margarine. Add turkey, mushrooms and bell pepper. Sauté 5 minutes or until turkey is no longer pink inside. Remove from skillet; set aside.

2. In same skillet, bring 1⅓ cups water and milk to a boil.

3. Stir in pasta and Special Seasonings. Reduce heat to medium. Gently boil uncovered, 4 to 5 minutes or until pasta is tender. Stir in turkey mixture. Let stand 3 minutes before serving. *Makes 4 servings*

Prep Time: 10 minutes
Cook Time: 15 minutes

Tip: To make slicing easier, place turkey or chicken in the freezer for 10 minutes.

The most familiar sweet pepper is the green pepper, also known as the
bell pepper for its bell-like shape. Green peppers are picked before they ripen.
When ripe, a bell pepper is red, yellow, orange, white or purple, depending
on the variety. They are sweeter and crisper than green peppers.

Enticing Enchiladas

1 tablespoon vegetable oil

1 green or red bell pepper, chopped

½ cup chopped onion

4 cloves garlic, minced

1 package JENNIE-O TURKEY STORE® Lean Ground Turkey

1 tablespoon Mexican seasoning or chili powder

2 cans (10 ounces) mild enchilada sauce, divided

2 cups (8 ounces) shredded Mexican cheese blend or Monterey Jack cheese, divided

12 (7-inch) soft flour tortillas or flavored flour tortillas

1 cup shredded lettuce

½ cup diced tomato

   Ripe avocado slices (optional)

Heat oven to 375°F. Heat oil in large skillet over medium heat. Add bell pepper, onion and garlic; cook 5 minutes, stirring occasionally. Crumble turkey into skillet; sprinkle with seasoning. Cook about 8 minutes or until no longer pink, stirring occasionally. Stir in ½ cup enchilada sauce. Remove from heat; stir in 1 cup cheese. Spread ½ cup enchilada sauce over bottom of 13×9-inch baking dish. Spoon about ⅓ cup turkey mixture down center of each tortilla. Fold bottom of tortilla up over filling, fold in sides and roll up. Place seam side down in prepared dish. Spoon remaining enchilada sauce evenly over enchiladas. Cover with foil; bake 20 minutes. Sprinkle with remaining 1 cup cheese. Return to oven; bake, uncovered, 10 minutes or until cheese is melted and sauce is bubbly. Garnish with lettuce and tomato. Top with avocado, if desired. *Makes 6 servings*

Prep Time: 30 minutes
Cook Time: 45 minutes

Enticing Enchiladas

Silly Spaghetti Casserole

8 ounces uncooked spaghetti, broken in half
¼ cup finely grated Parmesan cheese
¼ cup cholesterol-free egg substitute
¾ pound lean ground turkey
⅓ cup chopped onion
½ (10-ounce) package frozen cut spinach, thawed and squeezed dry
2 cups pasta sauce
¾ cup (3 ounces) shredded part-skim mozzarella cheese
1 red and/or yellow bell pepper, cored and seeded

1. Preheat oven to 350°F. Spray 8-inch square baking dish with nonstick cooking spray.

2. Cook spaghetti according to package directions, omitting salt and oil; drain. Return spaghetti to saucepan. Add Parmesan cheese and egg substitute; toss. Place in prepared baking dish.

3. Spray large nonstick skillet with cooking spray. Cook turkey and onion in skillet over medium-high heat until meat is lightly browned, stirring to break up meat. Drain fat from skillet. Stir in spinach and pasta sauce. Spoon over spaghetti mixture. Sprinkle with mozzarella cheese.

4. Use small cookie cutter to cut decorative shapes from bell pepper. Arrange on top of cheese. Cover with foil. Bake 40 to 45 minutes or until bubbling. Let stand 10 minutes. Cut into squares. *Makes 6 servings*

Developed for use in commercial and food service applications, processed liquid egg products are now available in cholesterol-free versions for the retail consumer. They are available refrigerated and frozen. Cholesterol-free products generally contain egg whites, nonfat milk, emulsifiers, stabilizers, gums and color. These products can be substituted for whole eggs in cooking and baking. Pasteurized liquid eggs that contain both whites and yolks are also available. Although these are not cholesterol-free, they are a good choice for use in lightly cooked egg dishes or homemade eggnog.

Silly Spaghetti Casserole

Wild Rice Meatball Primavera

   1 pound ground turkey
   ½ cup seasoned bread crumbs
   1 egg, beaten
   2 tablespoons oil
   1 can (10¾ ounces) condensed cream of mushroom soup, undiluted
   2 cups water
   1 package (16 ounces) frozen broccoli medley, thawed
   1 box UNCLE BEN'S® Long Grain & Wild Rice Fast Cook Recipe

1. Combine turkey, bread crumbs and egg; mix well. Shape into 1¼- to 1½-inch meatballs (about 20 to 22 meatballs).

2. Heat oil in large skillet over medium-high heat until hot. Cook meatballs 6 to 7 minutes or until brown on all sides. Drain on paper towels.

3. Combine soup and water in skillet; bring to a boil. Add meatballs, vegetables and contents of seasoning packet, reserving rice. Cover; reduce heat and simmer 5 minutes, stirring occasionally.

4. Add reserved rice to skillet; mix well. Cover; cook 5 minutes more or until hot. Remove from heat; stir well. Cover and let stand 5 minutes before serving.

Makes 6 servings

Classic Turkey Pot Pie

   2 cans (15 ounces each) VEG•ALL® Original Mixed Vegetables, drained
   1 can (10¾ ounces) cream of potato soup, undiluted
   ¼ cup milk
   1 pound cooked turkey, shredded (2 cups)
   ¼ teaspoon dried thyme
   ¼ teaspoon black pepper
   2 (9-inch) refrigerated ready-to-bake pie crusts

Preheat oven to 375°F. In medium mixing bowl, combine first 6 ingredients; mix well. Place 1 pie crust into 9-inch pie pan; pour vegetable mixture into pie crust. Top with remaining crust, crimp edges to seal, and slit top with knife. Bake for 50 to 60 minutes (on lower rack) or until crust is golden brown and filling is hot. Allow pie to cool slightly before cutting into wedges to serve.

Makes 8 servings

Wild Rice Meatball Primavera

Southwestern Turkey Stew

1 tablespoon vegetable oil
1 small onion, finely chopped
1 clove garlic, minced
2 cups low-sodium chicken broth
2 cups cooked smoked turkey breast, cut into ½-inch pieces
2 cups frozen corn kernels
1 can (about 14 ounces) diced tomatoes
1 package (about 6 ounces) red beans and rice mix
1 to 2 chipotle peppers in adobo sauce,* drained and minced
   Chopped green onion (optional)

Canned chipotle peppers can be found in the Mexican section of most supermarkets or gourmet food stores.

1. Heat oil in large nonstick skillet over medium-high heat. Add onion and garlic; cook and stir 3 minutes or until onion is translucent.

2. Add broth; bring to a boil. Stir in turkey, corn, tomatoes, bean mix and chipotle pepper. Reduce heat to low. Cover; cook 10 to 12 minutes or until rice is tender. Let stand 3 minutes. Garnish with green onion.   *Makes 4 servings*

Substitutions: Use 1 can (about 14 ounces) diced tomatoes with jalapeño peppers or ¼ teaspoon chipotle chili powder and 1 minced jalapeño pepper in place of the chipotle pepper.

Chipotle peppers are smoked jalapeños. They are usually found canned in adobo sauce, which is a dark red Mexican-style sauce made of chile peppers, herbs and vinegar. Store leftover canned chipotle peppers in adobo sauce in a foodsafe container in the freezer for later use.

Southwestern Turkey Stew

Chipotle Tamale Pie

¾ **pound ground turkey**
 1 **cup chopped onion**
¾ **cup diced green bell pepper**
¾ **cup diced red bell pepper**
 4 **cloves garlic, minced**
 2 **teaspoons ground cumin**
 1 **can (15 ounces) pinto or red beans, rinsed and drained**
 1 **can (8 ounces) no-salt-added stewed tomatoes, undrained**
 2 **canned chipotle chiles in adobo sauce, minced (about 1 tablespoon)**
 1 **to 2 teaspoons adobo sauce from canned chiles (optional)**
 1 **cup (4 ounces) shredded Cheddar cheese**
½ **cup chopped fresh cilantro**
 1 **package (8½ ounces) corn bread mix**
⅓ **cup milk**
 1 **large egg white**

1. Preheat oven to 400°F.

2. Cook turkey, onion, bell peppers and garlic in large nonstick skillet over medium-high heat 8 minutes or until browned, stirring occasionally. Drain fat. Sprinkle turkey mixture with cumin.

3. Add beans, tomatoes with juice, chiles and adobo sauce, if desired; bring to a boil over high heat. Reduce heat to medium; simmer, uncovered, 5 minutes. Remove from heat; stir in cheese and cilantro.

4. Spray 8-inch square baking dish with nonstick cooking spray. Spoon turkey mixture evenly into prepared dish, pressing down to compact mixture.

5. Combine corn bread mix, milk and egg white in medium bowl; stir just until dry ingredients are moistened. Spoon batter evenly over turkey mixture to cover completely.

6. Bake 20 to 22 minutes or until corn bread is golden brown. Let stand 5 minutes before serving.

Makes 6 servings

Chipotle Tamale Pie

Turkey and Mushroom Wild Rice Casserole

2 tablespoons butter
1 cup sliced mushrooms *or* 1 can (4 ounces) sliced mushrooms
1 small onion, chopped
1 stalk celery, chopped
1 can (about 10 ounces) condensed cream of mushroom soup, undiluted
1 pouch (about 9 ounces) ready-to-serve wild rice
2 cups diced cooked turkey breast
1 cup milk
2 tablespoons minced fresh chives
¼ teaspoon black pepper
½ cup coarsely chopped pecans

Preheat oven to 350°F. Melt butter in large nonstick skillet over medium heat. Add mushrooms, onion and celery; cook 5 minutes or until onion is translucent. Stir in soup, rice, turkey, milk, chives and pepper; mix well. Spoon mixture into 2-quart baking dish. Sprinkle with pecans. Bake 15 to 18 minutes or until hot and bubbly.   *Makes 4 servings*

Turkey and Stuffing Bake

1 jar (4½ ounces) sliced mushrooms
¼ cup butter or margarine
½ cup *each* diced celery and chopped onion
1¼ cups HIDDEN VALLEY® The Original Ranch® Salad Dressing, divided
⅔ cup water
3 cups seasoned stuffing mix
⅓ cup sweetened dried cranberries
3 cups coarsely shredded cooked turkey (about 1 pound)

Drain mushrooms, reserving liquid; set aside. Melt butter over medium-high heat in a large skillet. Add celery and onion; sauté for 4 minutes or until soft. Remove from heat and stir in ½ cup dressing, water and reserved mushroom liquid. Stir in stuffing mix and cranberries until thoroughly moistened. Mix turkey, mushrooms and remaining ¾ cup dressing in a separate bowl; spread evenly in a greased 8-inch baking dish. Top with stuffing mixture. Bake at 350°F for 40 minutes or until bubbly and brown.   *Makes 4 to 6 servings*

Turkey and Mushroom Wild Rice Casserole

Turkey Vegetable Crescent Pie

2 cans (about 14 ounces each) reduced-sodium chicken broth
1 medium onion, diced
1¼ pounds turkey tenderloins, cut into ¾-inch pieces
3 cups diced red potatoes
1 teaspoon chopped fresh rosemary *or* ½ teaspoon dried rosemary
¼ teaspoon salt
⅛ teaspoon black pepper
1 bag (16 ounces) frozen mixed vegetables
1 bag (10 ounces) frozen mixed vegetables
⅓ cup milk, plus additional if necessary
3 tablespoons cornstarch
1 package (8 ounces) refrigerated crescent rolls

1. Bring broth to a boil in large saucepan. Add onion; reduce heat and simmer 3 minutes. Add turkey; return to a boil. Reduce heat; cover and simmer 7 to 9 minutes or until turkey is no longer pink. With slotted spoon, transfer turkey to 13×9-inch baking dish.

2. Return broth to a boil. Add potatoes, rosemary, salt and pepper; simmer 2 minutes. Return to a boil; stir in mixed vegetables. Simmer, covered, 7 to 8 minutes or until potatoes are tender. With slotted spoon remove vegetables to colander set over bowl; reserve broth. Transfer vegetables to baking dish with turkey.

3. Preheat oven to 375°F. Blend ⅓ cup milk and cornstarch in small bowl until smooth; set aside. Add enough additional milk to reserved broth to equal 3 cups. Heat in large saucepan over medium-high heat. Whisk in cornstarch mixture, stirring constantly until mixture comes to a boil. Boil 1 minute; remove from heat. Pour over turkey-vegetable mixture in baking dish.

4. Roll out crescent roll dough and separate at perforations; arrange dough pieces decoratively over top of turkey-vegetable mixture. Bake 13 to 15 minutes or until crust is golden brown.   *Makes 8 servings*

Turkey Vegetable Crescent Pie

Creamy Turkey & Broccoli

1 package (6 ounces) stuffing mix, plus ingredients to prepare mix*
1⅓ cups *French's*® French Fried Onions, divided
1 package (10 ounces) frozen broccoli spears, thawed and drained
1 package (about 1⅛ ounces) cheese sauce mix
1¼ cups milk
½ cup sour cream
2 cups (10 ounces) cubed cooked turkey or chicken

*3 cups leftover stuffing can be substituted for stuffing mix. If stuffing is dry, stir in water, 1 tablespoon at a time, until moist but not wet.

Preheat oven to 350°F. In medium saucepan, prepare stuffing mix according to package directions; stir in ⅔ *cup* French Fried Onions. Spread stuffing over bottom of greased 9-inch round baking dish. Arrange broccoli spears over stuffing with flowerets around edge of dish. In medium saucepan, prepare cheese sauce mix according to package directions using 1¼ cups milk. Remove from heat; stir in sour cream and turkey. Pour turkey mixture over broccoli stalks. Bake, covered, at 350°F for 30 minutes or until heated through. Sprinkle remaining ⅔ *cup* onions over turkey; bake, uncovered, 5 minutes or until onions are golden brown.   *Makes 4 to 6 servings*

Microwave Directions: In 9-inch round microwave-safe dish, prepare stuffing mix according to package microwave directions; stir in ⅔ *cup* French Fried Onions. Arrange stuffing and broccoli spears in dish as above; set aside. In medium microwave-safe bowl, prepare cheese sauce mix according to package microwave directions using 1¼ cups milk. Add turkey and microwave, covered, on HIGH 5 to 6 minutes, stirring turkey halfway through cooking time. Stir in sour cream. Pour turkey mixture over broccoli stalks. Microwave, covered, 8 to 10 minutes or until heated through. Rotate dish halfway through cooking time. Top turkey with remaining ⅔ *cup* onions; microwave, uncovered, 1 minute. Let stand 5 minutes.

Cutting foods into uniform shapes and sizes results in more even cooking. In general, foods that will be microwaved should be cut smaller than food that is to be cooked by other methods.

Turkey Breast Provençal with Vegetables

1 cup turkey or reduced-sodium chicken broth
¼ cup dry white wine
¼ cup lemon juice
1 head garlic, cloves separated, unpeeled
1 bag (10 ounces) frozen onions
2 teaspoons dried rosemary, crushed
1 teaspoon dried thyme leaves
½ teaspoon salt
¼ teaspoon fennel seeds, crushed
¼ teaspoon black pepper
6 plum tomatoes, quartered
1 package (9 ounces) frozen artichoke hearts, slightly thawed
1 package (10 ounces) frozen asparagus spears, slightly thawed
1 can (3¼ ounces) pitted ripe olives, drained
1 bone-in (4½-pound) turkey breast

1. Preheat oven to 325°F. In 13×9-inch baking pan combine broth, wine, lemon juice, garlic, onions, rosemary, thyme, salt, fennel seeds and black pepper. Cover pan with foil; bake 20 minutes.

2. Remove pan from oven. Add tomatoes, artichoke hearts, asparagus and olives in a pile in the center of the pan. Place turkey breast on top of vegetables. Loosely tent with foil and roast 1 hour. Remove foil and roast 1 hour or until meat thermometer inserted in thickest part of breast registers 170°F. Baste turkey and vegetables frequently with pan juices.

3. Remove turkey and vegetables to serving platter. Reserve 6 cloves of garlic and pan juices.

4. Remove skin from reserved garlic. Combine garlic with pan juices in food processor; process 30 to 60 seconds until mixture is smooth. Reheat sauce to piping hot.

5. Serve sauce with turkey and vegetables.   *Makes 12 servings*

Favorite recipe from **National Turkey Federation**

Oriental Stir-Fry

1 bag SUCCESS® Rice
    Spicy Oriental Sauce (recipe follows)
¼ cup safflower oil, divided
¾ pound skinless, boneless turkey, cut into strips
½ teaspoon minced fresh ginger
1 clove garlic, minced
1 cup broccoli florets
1 medium onion, cut into wedges
1 yellow bell pepper, seeded and cut into strips
2 medium tomatoes, each cut into 6 wedges

Prepare rice according to package directions.

Prepare Spicy Oriental Sauce; set aside.

Heat 2 tablespoons oil in large skillet or wok. Add turkey, ginger and garlic; stir-fry until turkey is no longer pink in center. Remove turkey from skillet; set aside.

Heat remaining 2 tablespoons oil in same skillet. Add broccoli, onion and bell pepper; stir-fry 1 minute. Return turkey to skillet with tomatoes. Stir sauce; add to skillet. Cook and stir until sauce is thickened. Serve over hot rice. Garnish, if desired.   *Makes 4 servings*

Spicy Oriental Sauce

2 tablespoons cornstarch
½ cup water
2 tablespoons reduced-sodium soy sauce
1 tablespoon sherry
1 tablespoon Worcestershire sauce
1 teaspoon curry powder

Combine all ingredients in small bowl; mix well.

Oriental Stir-Fry

Turkey Meatball & Olive Casserole

2 cups uncooked rotini
½ pound ground turkey
¼ cup dry bread crumbs
1 egg, lightly beaten
2 teaspoons dried minced onion
2 teaspoons white wine Worcestershire sauce
½ teaspoon Italian seasoning
½ teaspoon salt
⅛ teaspoon black pepper
1 tablespoon vegetable oil
1 can (about 10 ounces) condensed cream of celery soup, undiluted
½ cup plain yogurt
¾ cup pimiento-stuffed green olives, sliced
3 tablespoons Italian-style bread crumbs
1 tablespoon butter, melted
Paprika (optional)

1. Preheat oven to 350°F. Spray 2-quart round casserole with nonstick cooking spray.

2. Cook pasta according to package directions until al dente. Drain and set aside.

3. Meanwhile, combine turkey, dry bread crumbs, egg, onion, Worcestershire, Italian seasoning, salt and pepper in medium bowl. Shape mixture into ½-inch meatballs.

4. Heat oil in medium skillet over high heat until hot. Add meatballs in single layer; cook until lightly browned on all sides and still pink in centers, turning frequently. Do not overcook. Remove from skillet; drain on paper towels.

5. Combine soup and yogurt in large bowl. Add pasta, meatballs and olives; stir gently to combine. Transfer to prepared dish.

6. Combine Italian-style bread crumbs and butter in small bowl; sprinkle evenly over casserole. Sprinkle lightly with paprika, if desired.

7. Bake, covered, 30 minutes. Uncover and bake 12 minutes or until meatballs are no longer pink in centers and casserole is hot and bubbly.

Makes 6 to 8 servings

Turkey & Green Bean Casserole

¼ cup slivered almonds

1 package (7 ounces) herb-seasoned stuffing cubes

¾ cup reduced-sodium chicken broth

1 can (about 10 ounces) condensed cream of mushroom soup, undiluted

¼ cup milk or half and half

¼ teaspoon black pepper

1 package (10 ounces) frozen French-style green beans, thawed and drained

2 cups cubed cooked cooked turkey

1. Preheat oven to 350°F. Spray 11×7-inch baking dish with nonstick cooking spray; set aside.

2. Spread almonds in single layer on baking sheet. Bake 5 minutes or until golden brown, stirring frequently. Set aside.

3. Arrange stuffing cubes in prepared dish; drizzle with broth. Stir to coat bread cubes with broth.

4. Combine soup, milk and pepper in large bowl. Add green beans and turkey; stir until blended. Spoon over stuffing cubes; top with almonds. Bake, uncovered, 30 to 35 minutes or until heated through.   *Makes 4 servings*

The next time you're making a casserole, assemble and bake two. Allow one to cool completely, then wrap it in heavy-duty foil and freeze it for another day. To reheat a frozen 2-quart casserole, unwrap it and microwave, covered, on HIGH for 20 to 30 minutes, stirring once or twice during cooking. Let the casserole stand about 5 minutes before serving.

Turkey & Green Bean Casserole

Stir-Fried Turkey with Broccoli

2 tablespoons lemon juice
   Peel of 1 lemon, grated
1 teaspoon dried thyme
½ teaspoon salt
¼ teaspoon white pepper
1 pound turkey cutlets, cut into strips
4 cups water
1 pound fresh broccoli, florets separated and stems cut into 2-inch pieces
1 cup chicken broth
1 tablespoon cornstarch
3 tablespoons vegetable oil, divided
1 tablespoon butter
¼ pound fresh button mushrooms, sliced
1 medium red onion, sliced and separated into rings
1 can (14 ounces) pre-cut baby corn, rinsed and drained*
   Hot cooked rice

Or, substitute 15-ounce can whole baby corn, cut into 1-inch lengths.

1. Combine lemon juice, peel, thyme, salt and pepper in small bowl. Add turkey to lemon mixture; coat well. Marinate 30 minutes.

2. Place 4 cups water in wok; bring to a boil over medium-high heat. Add broccoli stems; cook 1 minute. Add florets; cook 2 minutes more or until crisp-tender. Drain; rinse with cold water.

3. Stir chicken broth into cornstarch in cup until dissolved; set aside.

4. Heat wok over medium-high heat. Add 1 tablespoon oil and butter; heat until hot. Add mushrooms; stir-fry 2 minutes. Add onion; stir-fry 2 minutes. Remove to large bowl.

5. Heat 1 tablespoon oil in wok. Fry half of turkey strips in single layer 1½ minutes or until well browned. Transfer to mushroom mixture. Repeat with remaining 1 tablespoon oil and turkey.

6. Add baby corn to wok and heat 1 minute. Stir cornstarch mixture; add to wok and cook until bubbly. Add turkey, broccoli, mushrooms and onion; cook and stir until heated through. Serve over rice. *Makes 4 to 6 servings*

Stir-Fried Turkey with Broccoli

Rice Lasagna

1 bag SUCCESS® Rice
  Vegetable cooking spray
2 tablespoons reduced-calorie margarine
1 pound ground turkey
1 cup chopped onion
1 cup sliced fresh mushrooms
1 clove garlic, minced
2 cans (8 ounces each) no-salt-added tomato sauce
1 can (6 ounces) no-salt-added tomato paste
1 teaspoon dried oregano leaves, crushed
1 carton (15 ounces) lowfat cottage cheese
½ cup (2 ounces) grated Parmesan cheese
2 cups (8 ounces) shredded mozzarella cheese
1 tablespoon dried parsley flakes

Prepare rice according to package directions.

Preheat oven to 350°F.

Spray 13×9-inch baking dish with cooking spray; set aside. Melt margarine in large skillet over medium heat. Add ground turkey, onion, mushrooms and garlic; cook until turkey is no longer pink and vegetables are tender, stirring occasionally to separate turkey. Drain. Stir in tomato sauce, tomato paste and oregano; simmer 15 minutes, stirring occasionally. Layer half each of rice, turkey mixture, cottage cheese, Parmesan cheese and mozzarella cheese in prepared baking dish; repeat layers. Sprinkle with parsley; cover. Bake 30 minutes. Uncover; continue baking 15 minutes. *Makes 8 servings*

*Fresh ground turkey is sold in most supermarkets and can be used
in place of ground beef in many recipes. It has soared in popularity due
to a lower fat content. Read the label carefully; if skin or fat is ground
along with the meat, the amount of fat and cholesterol will increase.*

Rice Lasagna

Turnip Shepherd's Pie

1 pound small turnips,* peeled and cut into ½-inch cubes
1 pound ground turkey
⅓ cup dry bread crumbs
¼ cup chopped onion
¼ cup ketchup
1 egg
½ teaspoon salt
½ teaspoon Beau Monde seasoning**
½ teaspoon black pepper
⅓ cup half-and-half
1 tablespoon butter
1 tablespoon chopped fresh parsley
¼ cup (1 ounce) shredded sharp Cheddar cheese

For Rutabaga Shepherd's Pie, use 1 pound rutabagas in place of turnips.

**Beau Monde is a seasoning salt available in most supermarkets. Celery salt can be substituted.*

1. Preheat oven to 400°F. Place turnips in large saucepan; cover with water. Cover and bring to a boil; reduce heat to medium-low. Simmer 20 minutes or until fork-tender.

2. Combine turkey, bread crumbs, onion, ketchup, egg, salt and pepper in large bowl; mix well. Pat onto bottom and up side of 9-inch pie pan. Bake 20 to 30 minutes or until turkey is no longer pink. Blot with paper towel to remove any drippings.

3. Drain cooked turnips. Mash turnips until smooth. Add half-and-half and butter; stir until well blended. Season to taste with additional salt and pepper. Fill meat shell with turnip mixture; sprinkle with parsley and cheese. Return to oven until cheese melts.

Makes 4 servings

Turnip Shepherd's Pie

Southern Pork Barbecue Dinner

1 tablespoon vegetable oil
½ cup chopped onion
½ cup chopped celery
½ cup chopped green bell pepper
1 container (about 18 ounces) refrigerated
    fully cooked shredded pork
1 can (15 ounces) pinto beans or black-eyed
    peas, rinsed and drained
1 can (8 ounces) tomato sauce
2 tablespoons Dijon mustard

1. Heat oil in large skillet over medium-high heat. Add onion, celery and bell pepper; cook and stir 5 minutes or until tender.

2. Stir in pork, beans, tomato sauce and mustard. Cook over low heat 5 to 10 minutes or until hot.

Makes 4 to 6 servings

Variation: To make a sandwich, omit the beans and serve on buns.

Southern Pork Barbecue Dinner

Honey Nut Stir-Fry

1 pound pork steak, pork loin or boneless chicken breast
¾ cup orange juice
⅓ cup honey
3 tablespoons soy sauce
1 tablespoon cornstarch
¼ teaspoon ground ginger
2 tablespoons vegetable oil, divided
2 large carrots, sliced diagonally
2 stalks celery, sliced diagonally
½ cup cashews or peanuts
    Hot cooked rice

Cut pork into thin strips; set aside. Combine orange juice, honey, soy sauce, cornstarch and ginger in small bowl; mix well. Heat 1 tablespoon oil in large skillet over medium-high heat. Add carrots and celery; stir-fry about 3 minutes. Remove vegetables; set aside. Pour remaining 1 tablespoon oil into skillet. Add pork; stir-fry about 3 minutes. Return vegetables to skillet; add honey mixture and nuts. Cook and stir over medium-high heat until sauce comes to a boil and thickens. Serve over rice.   *Makes 4 to 6 servings*

Favorite recipe from **National Honey Board**

Honey is one of the only foods that will never go bad, no mater how long you keep it. Be sure to store it in a cool, dry and dark place in a tightly sealed jar. Do not refrigerate honey as it will become grainy and too thick to use.

Sausage and Broccoli Noodle Casserole

1 jar (1 pound) RAGÚ® Cheesy! Classic Alfredo Sauce
⅓ cup milk
1 pound sweet Italian sausage, cooked and crumbled
1 package (9 ounces) frozen chopped broccoli, thawed
8 ounces egg noodles, cooked and drained
1 cup shredded Cheddar cheese (about 4 ounces), divided
¼ cup chopped roasted red peppers

1. Preheat oven to 350°F. In large bowl, combine Alfredo Sauce and milk. Stir in sausage, broccoli, noodles, ¾ cup cheese and roasted peppers.

2. In 13×9-inch baking dish, evenly spread sausage mixture. Sprinkle with remaining ¼ cup cheese.

3. Bake 30 minutes or until heated through.   *Makes 6 servings*

Prep Time: 15 minutes
Cook Time: 30 minutes

Tip: Substitute sausage with equal amounts of vegetables for a hearty vegetarian entrée.

*Natural cheeses are categorized by the amount of moisture
they contain. Categories include hard cheese, such as Parmesan, with
30 percent moisture; firm, such as Cheddar, with 30 to 40 percent moisture;
semisoft, such as Monterey Jack, with 40 to 50 percent moisture; soft and
ripened, such as Brie, with 50 to 75 percent moisture; and soft and
unripened, such as cream cheese, with 80 percent moisture.*

Sausage and Broccoli Noodle Casserole

New Orleans Rice and Sausage

½ pound smoked sausage,* cut into slices
1 can (14½ ounces) Cajun- or Italian-style stewed tomatoes
¾ cup water
1¾ cups uncooked instant rice
    Dash TABASCO®** brand Pepper Sauce or to taste
1 bag (16 ounces) BIRDS EYE® frozen Broccoli, Corn and Red Peppers

For a spicy dish, use andouille sausage. Any type of kielbasa or turkey kielbasa can also be used.

**Tabasco® is a registered trademark of McIlhenny Company.*

• Heat sausage in large skillet 2 to 3 minutes.

• Add tomatoes, water, rice and TABASCO® Pepper Sauce; mix well.

• Add vegetables; mix well. Cover and cook over medium heat 5 to 7 minutes or until rice is tender and vegetables are heated through.   *Makes 6 servings*

Vegetable Pork Stir-Fry

¾ pound pork tenderloin
1 tablespoon vegetable oil
1½ cups (about 6 ounces) sliced fresh mushrooms
1 large green bell pepper, cut into strips
1 zucchini, thinly sliced
2 stalks celery, cut into diagonal slices
1 cup thinly sliced carrots
1 clove garlic, minced
1 cup chicken broth
2 tablespoons reduced-sodium soy sauce
1½ tablespoons cornstarch
3 cups hot cooked rice

Slice pork across the grain into ⅛-inch strips. Brown pork strips in oil in large skillet over medium-high heat. Push meat to side of skillet. Add mushrooms, pepper, zucchini, celery, carrots and garlic; stir-fry about 3 minutes. Combine broth, soy sauce and cornstarch. Add to skillet and cook, stirring, until thickened; cook 1 minute longer. Serve over rice.   *Makes 6 servings*

*Favorite recipe from **USA Rice***

New Orleans Rice and Sausage

Pork and Vegetable Stew with Noodles

2 tablespoons vegetable oil

1 pound boneless pork sirloin steaks, cut into ¾-inch cubes or pork for stew

3 cups beef broth

3 tablespoons chopped fresh parsley, divided

1 can (about 14 ounces) stewed tomatoes, undrained

1 large carrot, sliced

3 green onions, sliced

2 teaspoons Dijon mustard

¼ teaspoon rubbed sage

⅛ teaspoon black pepper

3 cups uncooked noodles

1 teaspoon butter

⅓ cup cold water

2 tablespoons all-purpose flour

1. Heat oil in large saucepan over medium-high heat. Add meat; brown, stirring frequently. Gradually add beef broth. Stir in 1 tablespoon chopped parsley, tomatoes with juice, carrot, onions, mustard, sage and pepper. Bring to a boil over high heat. Reduce heat to medium-low; simmer, uncovered, 30 minutes.

2. Meanwhile, cook noodles according to package directions; drain and place in bowl. Add remaining 2 tablespoons chopped parsley and butter; toss lightly. Keep warm until ready to serve.

3. Stir cold water into flour in cup until smooth. Stir into stew. Cook and stir over medium heat until slightly thickened. To serve, spoon noodles onto each plate. Ladle stew over noodles. Garnish, if desired.   *Makes 4 servings*

Pork and Vegetable Stew with Noodles

Thai Basil Pork Stir-Fry

  1 pound boneless pork tenderloin, sliced across the grain into ¼-inch
     slices
½ teaspoon crushed or minced garlic
  1 tablespoon soy sauce
  2 tablespoons canola oil
  1 pound bag ready-to-use pre-cut broccoli florets
  1 medium red bell pepper, cut into strips
  1 to 2 tablespoons Thai green curry paste (see Note)
1¼ cups chicken broth
  2 tablespoons chopped Italian or Thai basil leaves
  2 tablespoons finely chopped roasted peanuts
  3 cups fresh mung bean sprouts

1. In a small bowl, combine pork, garlic and soy sauce; toss to coat. Set pork aside.

2. Heat oil in 12-inch nonstick skillet over high heat. When pan is hot, add broccoli; stir-fry 3 to 4 minutes or until broccoli begins to brown but is not cooked through. Add bell pepper; stir-fry 1 minute. Add reserved pork mixture and curry paste; stir-fry 2 minutes more. Add chicken broth; cook and stir 2 to 3 minutes more or until heated through.

3. Remove from heat and stir in chopped basil.

4. To serve, spoon onto plates; sprinkle with 1 teaspoon chopped peanuts. Serve with bean sprouts.
Makes 6 servings

Note: Thai green curry paste is available in the ethnic section of most supermarkets in cans or jars. Use 1 tablespoon for a mildly spicy dish or 2 tablespoons for hot.

Thai Basil Pork Stir-Fry

Carolina Baked Beans & Pork Chops

2 cans (16 ounces each) pork and beans
½ cup chopped onion
½ cup chopped green bell pepper
¼ cup *French's® Classic Yellow®* Mustard
¼ cup packed light brown sugar
2 tablespoons *French's®* Worcestershire Sauce
1 tablespoon *Frank's® RedHot®* Original Cayenne Pepper Sauce
6 boneless pork chops (1 inch thick)

1. Preheat oven to 400°F. Combine all ingredients *except pork chops* in 3-quart shallow baking dish; mix well. Arrange chops on top, turning once to coat with sauce.

2. Bake, uncovered, 30 to 35 minutes or until pork is no longer pink in center. Stir beans around chops once during baking. Serve with green beans or mashed potatoes, if desired.

Makes 6 servings

Prep Time: 10 minutes
Cook Time: 30 minutes

Brown sugar is a mixture of granulated sugar and molasses that adds a rich flavor to baked goods. Dark brown sugar has more molasses added and will actually give foods a darker color. Light brown sugar has a milder flavor and lighter color than the dark variety. Whatever the type, brown sugar is moist and clingy when fresh but can easily dry out. Adding a slice of apple or bread to the box or bag will restore moisture.

Carolina Baked Beans & Pork Chop

Sesame Pork with Broccoli

1 can (14½ ounces) chicken broth
2 tablespoons cornstarch
1 tablespoon soy sauce
4 green onions with tops, finely diced
1 pound pork tenderloin, trimmed
1 tablespoon vegetable oil
1 clove garlic, minced
1½ pounds fresh broccoli, cut into bite-size pieces (about 7 cups)
2 tablespoons sliced pimiento, drained
Hot cooked rice (optional)
2 tablespoons sesame seeds, lightly toasted

Combine chicken broth, cornstarch and soy sauce in small bowl; blend well. Stir in green onions; set aside. Cut pork tenderloin lengthwise into quarters; cut each quarter into bite-size pieces. Heat oil in wok or heavy skillet over medium-high heat. Add pork and garlic; stir-fry 3 to 4 minutes or until pork is tender. Remove pork; keep warm. Stir broth mixture; add to wok with broccoli. Cover and simmer over low heat 8 minutes. Add cooked pork and pimiento to wok; cook just until mixture is hot, stirring frequently. Serve over rice, if desired. Sprinkle with sesame seeds. Garnish as desired.   *Makes 6 servings*

Favorite recipe from **National Pork Board**

*To toast sesame seeds, spread the seeds in a small skillet.
Shake the skillet over medium heat for about 2 minutes
or until the seeds begin to pop and turn golden.*

Old-Fashioned Cabbage Rolls

½ pound ground beef
½ pound ground veal
½ pound ground pork
1 small onion, chopped
2 eggs, lightly beaten
½ cup dry bread crumbs
1 teaspoon salt
1 teaspoon molasses
¼ teaspoon ground ginger
¼ teaspoon ground nutmeg
¼ teaspoon ground allspice
1 large head cabbage, separated into leaves
3 cups boiling water
¼ cup butter
½ cup milk, plus additional if necessary
1 tablespoon cornstarch

1. Combine meats and onion in large bowl. Combine eggs, bread crumbs, salt, molasses, ginger, nutmeg and allspice in medium bowl; mix well. Add to meat mixture; stir until well blended.

2. Drop cabbage leaves into boiling water for 3 minutes. Remove with slotted spoon, reserving ½ cup of boiling liquid.

3. Preheat oven to 375°F. Place about 2 tablespoons meat mixture about 1 inch from stem end of each cabbage leaf. Fold sides in and roll up, fastening with toothpicks, if necessary.

4. Heat butter in large skillet over medium-high heat. Add cabbage rolls, 3 or 4 at a time, to skillet and brown on all sides. Arrange rolls, seam side down, in single layer in casserole. Combine reserved boiling liquid with butter remaining in skillet; pour over cabbage rolls.

5. Bake 1 hour. Carefully drain accumulated pan juices into measuring cup. Return cabbage rolls to oven. Add enough milk to pan juices to equal 1 cup.

6. Pour milk mixture into small saucepan. Stir in cornstarch; bring to a boil, stirring constantly until sauce is thickened. Pour over cabbage rolls. Bake 15 minutes more or until sauce is browned and cabbage is very tender.

Makes 8 servings

Teriyaki Rib Dinner

1 package (about 15 ounces) refrigerated fully cooked pork back ribs in barbecue sauce
2 tablespoons vegetable oil
1 large onion, thinly sliced
4 cups frozen Japanese-style stir-fry vegetables
1 can (8 ounces) pineapple chunks with juice
¼ cup hoisin sauce
2 tablespoons cider vinegar

1. Remove ribs from package; reserve extra barbecue sauce. Cut into individual ribs; set aside.

2. Heat oil in Dutch oven over medium-high heat. Add onion; cook 3 minutes or until translucent. Add vegetables; cook and stir 4 minutes.

3. Add ribs, reserved sauce, pineapple with juice, hoisin sauce and vinegar to vegetable mixture; mix well. Cover; cook 5 minutes or until hot.

Makes 4 servings

Spinach-Feta Rice & Ham

1 cup uncooked rice
1 cup reduced-sodium chicken broth
1 onion, chopped
1 cup sliced fresh mushrooms
2 cloves garlic, minced
1 tablespoon lemon juice
2 teaspoons chopped fresh oregano
6 cups (about ¼ pound) shredded fresh spinach leaves
1 cup chopped HILLSHIRE FARM® Ham
3 ounces feta cheese, crumbled
   Freshly ground black pepper

Combine rice, chicken broth and 1 cup water in medium saucepan over high heat. Bring to a boil; stir once or twice. Reduce heat; simmer, covered, 15 minutes or until rice is tender and liquid is absorbed. Spray large skillet with nonstick cooking spray. Sauté onion, mushrooms and garlic over medium-high heat until onion is tender. Stir in lemon juice and oregano. Add rice, spinach, Ham, cheese and pepper; toss lightly until spinach is wilted.

Makes 6 to 8 servings

Teriyaki Rib Dinner

Italian Tomato Bake

1 pound sweet Italian sausage, cut into ½-inch slices
2 tablespoons butter
1 cup chopped onion
4 cups cooked egg noodles
2 cups frozen broccoli florets, thawed and drained
2 cups prepared pasta sauce
½ cup diced plum tomatoes
2 cloves garlic, minced
3 plum tomatoes, sliced
1 cup (8 ounces) low-fat ricotta cheese
⅓ cup grated Parmesan cheese
1 teaspoon dried oregano

1. Preheat oven to 350°F. Cook sausage in large skillet over medium heat about 10 minutes or until barely pink in center. Drain on paper towels; set aside. Drain fat from skillet.

2. Add butter and onion to skillet; cook and stir until onion is tender. Combine onion, noodles, broccoli, pasta sauce, diced tomatoes and garlic in large bowl; mix well. Transfer to 13×9-inch baking dish.

3. Top with cooked sausage; arrange tomato slices on top. Place 1 heaping tablespoonful ricotta cheese on each tomato slice. Sprinkle with Parmesan cheese and oregano. Bake 35 minutes or until hot and bubbly.

Makes 6 servings

*The quickest way to peel garlic cloves is to trim off the ends
and crush the cloves with the flat side of a large knife or the bottom
of a heavy saucepan. The peels can then be easily removed.*

Italian Tomato Bake

Potato Sausage Casserole

1 pound bulk pork sausage or ground pork
1 can (10¾ ounces) condensed cream of mushroom soup, undiluted
¾ cup milk
½ cup chopped onion
½ teaspoon salt
¼ teaspoon black pepper
3 cups sliced potatoes
½ tablespoon butter, cut into small pieces
1½ cups (6 ounces) shredded Cheddar cheese

1. Preheat oven to 350°F. Spray 1½-quart casserole with nonstick cooking spray; set aside.

2. Cook sausage, stirring to separate, in large skillet over medium-high heat until no longer pink; drain fat.

3. Stir together soup, milk, onion, salt and pepper in medium bowl.

4. Place half of potatoes in prepared casserole. Top with half of soup mixture; top with half of sausage. Repeat layers, ending with sausage. Dot with butter.

5. Cover casserole with foil. Bake 1¼ to 1½ hours or until potatoes are tender. Uncover; sprinkle with cheese. Return to oven; bake until cheese is melted and casserole is bubbly. *Makes 6 servings*

Sunny Day Casserole

1 jar (8 ounces) pasteurized processed cheese spread, melted
¾ cup milk
4 cups diced potatoes, partially cooked
2 cups diced HILLSHIRE FARM® Ham
1 package (16 ounces) frozen mixed vegetables, thawed
½ cup chopped onion
1 cup (4 ounces) shredded Swiss, Cheddar or Monterey Jack cheese
1 cup cracker crumbs

Preheat oven to 350°F.

Combine cheese spread and milk in large bowl. Stir in potatoes, Ham, mixed vegetables and onion. Pour into medium casserole. Bake, covered, 45 minutes, stirring occasionally. Sprinkle cheese and cracker crumbs over top. Bake, uncovered, until cheese is melted. *Makes 6 servings*

Potato Sausage Casserole

Spicy Pork Chop Casserole

Nonstick cooking spray
2 cups frozen corn
2 cups frozen diced hash brown potatoes
1 can (about 14 ounces) diced tomatoes with basil, garlic and oregano, drained
2 teaspoons chili powder
1 teaspoon dried oregano
½ teaspoon ground cumin
⅛ teaspoon red pepper flakes
1 teaspoon olive oil
4 boneless pork loin chops (about 3 ounces each), cut about ¾ inch thick
¼ teaspoon black pepper
¼ cup (1 ounce) shredded Monterey Jack cheese (optional)

1. Preheat oven to 375°F.

2. Lightly spray nonstick skillet with cooking spray. Add corn; cook and stir over medium-high heat about 5 minutes or until corn begins to brown. Add potatoes; cook and stir about 5 minutes more or until potatoes begin to brown. Add tomatoes, chili powder, oregano, cumin and red pepper flakes; stir until blended.

3. Lightly spray 8×8×2-inch baking dish with cooking spray. Transfer corn mixture to prepared dish.

4. Wipe skillet with paper towel. Add oil and pork chops to skillet. Cook pork chops over medium-high heat until brown on one side. Remove pork chops; place browned side up on top of corn mixture in baking dish. Sprinkle with black pepper. Bake, uncovered, 20 minutes or until meat is juicy and barely pink in center. Sprinkle with cheese, if desired. Let stand 2 to 3 minutes before serving.

Makes 4 servings

Prep Time: 15 minutes
Bake Time: 20 minutes

Spicy Pork Chop Casserole

Easy Moroccan Casserole

2 tablespoons vegetable oil
1 pound pork stew meat, cut into 1-inch cubes
½ cup chopped onion
3 tablespoons all-purpose flour
1 can (about 14 ounces) diced tomatoes, undrained
¼ cup water
1 teaspoon ground ginger
1 teaspoon ground cumin
1 teaspoon ground cinnamon
½ teaspoon sugar
½ teaspoon salt
½ teaspoon black pepper
2 medium unpeeled red potatoes, cut into ½-inch pieces
1 large sweet potato, peeled and cut into ½-inch pieces
1 cup frozen lima beans, thawed and drained
1 cup frozen cut green beans, thawed and drained
¾ cup sliced carrots
   Pita bread

1. Preheat oven to 325°F.

2. Heat oil in large skillet over medium-high heat. Add pork and onion; cook until pork is browned on all sides, stirring occasionally. Sprinkle flour over meat mixture. Stir until flour has absorbed pan juices. Cook 2 minutes more.

3. Stir in tomatoes with juice, water, ginger, cumin, cinnamon, sugar, salt and pepper. Transfer mixture to 2-quart casserole. Bake 30 minutes.

4. Stir in red potatoes, sweet potato, lima beans, green beans and carrots. Cover; bake 1 hour or until potatoes are tender. Serve with pita bread.

Makes 6 servings

Easy Moroccan Casserole

Exotic Pork & Vegetables

¼ cup water
2 teaspoons cornstarch
4 tablespoons peanut oil, divided
6 whole dried hot red chili peppers
4 cloves garlic, sliced
1 pork tenderloin (about ¾ pound), thinly sliced
1 large carrot, peeled and cut into ¼-inch-thick slices*
2 ounces fresh oyster, shiitake or button mushrooms,** cut into halves
1 baby eggplant, thinly sliced
5 ounces fresh snow peas, ends trimmed
3 tablespoons packed brown sugar
2 tablespoons fish sauce
1 tablespoon dark sesame oil
Hot cooked rice

To make scalloped edges on carrot, use citrus stripper or grapefruit spoon to cut groove into carrot, cutting lengthwise from stem end to tip. Continue to cut grooves around carrot about ¼ inch apart. Then cut carrot crosswise into ¼-inch-thick slices.

**Or, substitute ½ ounce dried Oriental mushrooms, soaked according to package directions.*

1. Combine water and cornstarch in cup; set aside.

2. Heat wok or large skillet over high heat 1 minute. Drizzle 2 tablespoons peanut oil into wok and heat 30 seconds. Add peppers and garlic; stir-fry about 1 minute. Add pork; stir-fry 3 to 4 minutes or until no longer pink. Remove pork mixture to bowl; set aside.

3. Add remaining 2 tablespoons peanut oil to wok. Add carrot, mushrooms and eggplant; stir-fry 2 minutes. Add snow peas and pork mixture; stir-fry 1 minute.

4. Stir cornstarch mixture; add to wok. Cook 1 minute or until thickened. Stir in brown sugar, fish sauce and sesame oil; cook until heated through. Serve over rice.

Makes 4 servings

Exotic Pork & Vegetables

Normandy Pork and Cabbage

1 pound boneless pork loin or tenderloin
2 medium red baking apples, halved and cored
1 tablespoon vegetable oil
2 tablespoons butter, divided
1 package (8 ounces) shredded green cabbage for coleslaw *or* 2 cups
    shredded red cabbage
1 tablespoon all-purpose flour
1 teaspoon ground sage
½ teaspoon salt
¼ teaspoon black pepper
½ cup beef broth
½ cup apple juice or sweet apple cider
¼ cup heavy cream
    Hot cooked egg noodles

1. Trim fat from pork; discard. Cut pork crosswise into ¼-inch-thick slices. Cut each apple half into 6 wedges. Set aside.

2. Heat wok over high heat about 1 minute or until hot. Drizzle oil into wok and heat 30 seconds. Add 1 tablespoon butter and swirl to coat bottom. Add half the pork; stir-fry until well browned on both sides. Remove pork to large bowl. Repeat with remaining pork. Reduce heat to medium.

3. Add remaining 1 tablespoon butter to wok and swirl to coat bottom. Add apples; stir-fry about 2 minutes or just until apples soften. Remove apples to bowl with pork.

4. Add cabbage to wok; stir-fry just until wilted. Sprinkle with flour, sage, salt and black pepper; stir-fry until well mixed. Add broth and juice; cook and stir until sauce boils and thickens. Stir in cream; cook until heated through. Return pork and apples to wok. Stir in additional water if needed. Serve with noodles.

Makes 4 servings

Note: For best results, use Cortland, Rome Beauty, Winesap or Arkansas Black apples. They will remain flavorful and firm during cooking.

Ham and Potato au Gratin

        3 tablespoons butter or margarine
        3 tablespoons all-purpose flour
        2 cups milk
     1½ cups (6 ounces) shredded Cheddar cheese
        1 tablespoon Dijon mustard
        2 cups HILLSHIRE FARM® Ham, cut into thin strips
        1 package (24 ounces) frozen shredded hash brown potatoes, thawed
        1 package (10 ounces) frozen chopped spinach, thawed and drained

Preheat oven to 350°F.

Melt butter in large saucepan over medium heat; stir in flour. Add milk. Cook and stir until bubbly; cook 1 minute more. Remove from heat. Stir in cheese and mustard; set aside.

Place half of Ham in ungreased medium casserole. Top with half of potatoes and half of milk mixture. Spoon spinach over top. Repeat layers with remaining ham, potatoes and milk mixture.

Bake, uncovered, 30 minutes or until heated through.   *Makes 8 servings*

Italian-Glazed Pork Chops

        1 tablespoon olive oil
        8 bone-in pork chops
        1 medium zucchini, thinly sliced
        1 medium red bell pepper, chopped
        1 medium onion, thinly sliced
        3 cloves garlic, finely chopped
      ¼ cup dry red wine or beef broth
        1 jar (1 pound 10 ounces) RAGÚ® Chunky Pasta Sauce

1. In 12-inch skillet, heat olive oil over medium-high heat and brown chops. Remove chops and set aside.

2. In same skillet, cook zucchini, red bell pepper, onion and garlic, stirring occasionally, 4 minutes. Stir in wine and Ragú Pasta Sauce.

3. Return chops to skillet, turning to coat with sauce. Simmer covered 15 minutes or until chops are tender and barely pink in the center. Serve, if desired, over hot cooked couscous or rice.   *Makes 8 servings*

Prep Time: 10 minutes
Cook Time: 25 minutes

Spicy Lasagna Rollers

1½ pounds Italian sausage, casings removed
1 jar (28 ounces) spaghetti sauce, divided
1 can (8 ounces) tomato sauce
½ cup chopped roasted red pepper
¾ teaspoon dried Italian seasoning
½ teaspoon red pepper flakes
1 container (15 ounces) ricotta cheese
1 package (10 ounces) frozen chopped spinach, thawed and squeezed dry
2 cups (8 ounces) shredded Italian cheese blend, divided
1 cup (4 ounces) shredded Cheddar cheese, divided
1 egg, lightly beaten
12 lasagna noodles, cooked and drained

1. Preheat oven to 350°F. Spray 13×9-inch baking pan with nonstick cooking spray; set aside.

2. Cook sausage in large skillet over medium heat until browned, stirring to break up meat; drain. Stir in ½ cup spaghetti sauce, tomato sauce, roasted red pepper, Italian seasoning and pepper flakes.

3. Combine ricotta, spinach, 1½ cups Italian cheese blend , ½ cup Cheddar cheese and egg in medium bowl. Spread ¼ cup ricotta mixture over each noodle. Top with ⅓ cup sausage mixture. Tightly roll up each noodle from short end, jelly-roll style. Place rolls, seam sides down, in prepared pan. Pour remaining spaghetti sauce over rolls. Sprinkle with remaining ½ cup Italian cheese blend and ½ cup Cheddar cheese. Cover pan with foil.

4. Bake 30 minutes. Carefully remove foil; bake 15 minutes or until sauce is bubbly.

Makes 6 servings

Ricotta cheese resembles cottage cheese but is smoother, richer and creamier. It is prepared from whey left over from making mozzarella cheese. Like so many ingredients used in Italian cooking, it is inexpensive and readily available.

Spicy Lasagna Rollers

Mexicali Cornbread Casserole

2½ cups frozen mixed vegetables, thawed
1½ cups cubed HILLSHIRE FARM® Ham
  1 package (10 ounces) cornbread stuffing mix
  2 cups milk
  3 eggs, lightly beaten
    Salt and black pepper to taste
½ cup (2 ounces) shredded taco-flavored cheese

Preheat oven to 375°F.

Combine mixed vegetables, Ham and stuffing mix in small casserole; set aside. Combine milk, eggs, salt and pepper in medium bowl; pour over ham mixture. Bake, covered, 45 minutes. Top with cheese; bake, uncovered, 3 minutes or until cheese is melted. *Makes 4 servings*

Skillet Sausage and Bean Stew

  1 pound spicy Italian sausage, sliced ½ inch thick
½ onion, chopped
  2 cups frozen O'Brien hash brown potatoes with onions and peppers
  1 can (15 ounces) pinto beans, undrained
¾ cup water
  1 teaspoon beef bouillon granules *or* 1 beef bouillon cube
  1 teaspoon dried oregano
⅛ teaspoon ground red pepper

1. Combine sausage slices and onion in large nonstick skillet; cook and stir over medium-high heat 5 to 7 minutes or until meat is no longer pink. Drain drippings.

2. Stir in potatoes, beans, water, bouillon, oregano and red pepper; reduce heat to medium. Cover and simmer 15 minutes, stirring occasionally.

Makes 4 servings

Prep and Cook Time: 30 minutes

Tip: You can reduce the calories and fat content of this dish by substituting turkey sausage for Italian sausage. Add hot pepper sauce to taste if you prefer a spicier stew.

Mexicali Cornbread Casserole

Stuffed Green Peppers

6 medium to large green bell peppers
1 pound BOB EVANS® Original Recipe Roll Sausage
2 cups tomato sauce
2 cups water
1 small onion, chopped
1 cup uncooked rice
  Sliced green onion (optional)

Preheat oven to 350°F. Slice off tops from peppers; scrape out centers to remove seeds and membranes. Combine all remaining ingredients except green onion in medium bowl; mix well. Evenly stuff peppers with sausage mixture. Place in lightly greased deep 3-quart casserole dish. Bake, covered, 20 minutes. Uncover; bake 5 to 10 minutes more or until peppers are fork-tender and filling is set. Garnish with green onion, if desired. Serve hot. Refrigerate leftovers.

Makes 6 servings

Tip: For a pretty presentation, slice 6 small peppers lengthwise in half through stem; scrape out centers to remove seeds and membranes. Proceed as directed, serving 2 halves to each guest.

Serving Suggestion: Serve with mixed salad of carrot, radish and cucumber slices drizzled with a vinaigrette.

When choosing bell peppers, they should be firm, crisp and feel heavy for their size. They should be shiny and brightly colored and their stems should be green and hard. Avoid peppers that have wrinkles, soft spots or bruises. If you plan to stuff the peppers, purchase round, blocky peppers rather than oddly-shaped peppers.

Stuffed Green Peppers

SPAM™ *Hot & Spicy Stir-Fry*

⅓ cup reduced-sodium teriyaki sauce
⅓ cup water
2 to 3 teaspoons HOUSE OF TSANG® MONGOLIAN FIRE® Oil
½ teaspoon ground ginger
1 (12-ounce) can SPAM® Lite, cubed
1 cup broccoli florets
1 cup chopped onion
1 cup pea pods
1 red bell pepper, cut into strips
1 tablespoon plus 1½ teaspoons vegetable oil
1 (14-ounce) can whole baby corn, drained and cut in half
1 (7-ounce) jar mushrooms, drained
6 cups hot cooked white rice

In small bowl, combine teriyaki sauce, water, Chinese hot oil and ginger; set aside. In wok or large skillet, stir-fry SPAM®, broccoli, onion, pea pods and bell pepper in vegetable oil 2 minutes. Add teriyaki sauce mixture; cook until bubbly. Add baby corn and mushrooms; heat thoroughly. Serve over rice.

Makes 6 servings

*When purchasing fresh broccoli, choose bunches that are fresh-looking,
ranging in color from dark green to purple-green. The bud clusters should
be compact, showing no yellow color. Stalks and stems should also be
green and fresh-looking. Avoid bunches with wilted, yellowed leaves.*

SPAM™ *Hot & Spicy Stir-Fry*

Tuscan Baked Rigatoni

1 pound Italian sausage, casings removed
1 pound rigatoni pasta, cooked, drained and kept warm
2 cups (8 ounces) shredded fontina cheese
2 tablespoons olive oil
2 fennel bulbs, thinly sliced
4 cloves garlic, minced
1 can (28 ounces) crushed tomatoes
1 cup heavy cream
1 teaspoon salt
1 teaspoon black pepper
8 cups coarsely chopped fresh spinach
1 can (15 ounces) cannellini beans, rinsed and drained
2 tablespoons pine nuts
½ cup grated Parmesan cheese

1. Preheat oven to 350°F. Spray 4-quart casserole with nonstick cooking spray. Crumble sausage into large skillet over medium-high heat. Cook and stir until no longer pink; drain. Transfer sausage to large bowl. Add pasta and fontina cheese; mix well.

2. Combine oil, fennel and garlic in same skillet. Cook and stir over medium heat 3 minutes or until fennel is tender. Add tomatoes, cream, salt and pepper; cook and stir until slightly thickened. Stir in spinach, beans and pine nuts; cook until heated through.

3. Pour tomato sauce mixture over pasta and sausage; toss to coat. Transfer to prepared casserole; sprinkle evenly with Parmesan cheese. Bake 30 minutes or until hot and bubbly. *Makes 6 to 8 servings*

Tuscan Baked Rigatoni

Quick Cajun Jambalaya

    3 tablespoons butter
    1 onion, diced
    1 red bell pepper, diced
    1 green bell pepper, diced
   12 slices HILLSHIRE FARM® Ham, cut into ½-inch strips
   12 large raw shrimp, peeled and deveined
    1 can (28 ounces) crushed tomatoes, undrained
    2 teaspoons salt
   ¼ teaspoon garlic powder
   ¼ teaspoon red pepper flakes
   ¼ teaspoon black pepper
   ¼ teaspoon hot pepper sauce
    6 cups cooked white rice
      Cajun Garlic Bread (recipe follows)

Heat butter in large saucepan over medium-high heat; cook onion and bell peppers until soft, about 5 minutes. Add ham and shrimp; cook until shrimp turn pink, about 3 minutes. Add tomatoes with liquid, seasonings and rice; cook 5 minutes or until heated through. Serve with Cajun Garlic Bread.

Makes 6 servings

Cajun Garlic Bread

   ¼ teaspoon garlic powder
   ⅛ teaspoon ground red pepper
   ⅛ teaspoon dried oregano or basil leaves
    2 tablespoons butter, melted
    1 loaf French bread, cut lengthwise into halves

Preheat oven to 350°F. Stir garlic powder, red pepper and oregano into butter in small bowl. Drizzle butter mixture over cut sides of bread. Reassemble loaf; wrap in foil. Bake 10 minutes.

Makes 6 servings

*Quick Cajun Jambalaya and
Cajun Garlic Bread*

Stir-Fried Pork with Green Beans and Baby Corn

¾ pound pork tenderloin
1 tablespoon plus 1 teaspoon cornstarch, divided
2 tablespoons soy sauce
1 tablespoon rice wine or dry sherry
1 teaspoon sugar
½ teaspoon dark sesame oil
⅓ cup plus 2 tablespoons water, divided
2 tablespoons peanut oil, divided
1 pound fresh green beans, trimmed and cut into 1½-inch pieces
2 cloves garlic, minced
1 teaspoon finely chopped fresh ginger
1 tablespoon black bean sauce
1 can (14 ounces) baby corn, rinsed and drained

1. Slice pork across grain into thin slices; cut slices into ¾-inch strips.

2. Combine 1 teaspoon cornstarch, soy sauce, rice wine, sugar and sesame oil in medium bowl; mix well. Add pork; toss to coat. Set aside to marinate 20 to 30 minutes. Combine remaining 1 tablespoon cornstarch and ⅓ cup water in small bowl; set aside.

3. Heat 1 tablespoon peanut oil in wok or large skillet over high heat. Add beans; stir-fry about 4 minutes. Add remaining 2 tablespoons water; reduce heat to medium-low. Cover and simmer 10 to 12 minutes or until crisp-tender. Remove from wok; set aside.

4. Heat remaining 1 tablespoon peanut oil in wok over high heat. Add garlic, ginger and pork; stir-fry about 3 minutes or until meat is no longer pink. Add black bean sauce; stir-fry 1 minute.

5. Return beans to wok. Stir cornstarch mixture; add to wok. Bring to a boil; cook until sauce thickens. Stir in baby corn; heat through.   *Makes 4 servings*

*Stir-Fried Pork with Green Beans
and Baby Corn*

Italian Sausage Supper

1 pound mild Italian sausage, casing removed
1 cup chopped onion
3 medium zucchini, sliced (about 1½ cups)
1 can (6 ounces) CONTADINA® Tomato Paste
1 cup water
1 teaspoon dried basil leaves, crushed
½ teaspoon salt
3 cups cooked rice
1 cup (4 ounces) shredded mozzarella cheese
¼ cup (1 ounce) grated Romano cheese

1. Brown sausage with onion in large skillet, stirring to break up sausage; drain, reserving 1 tablespoon drippings.

2. Spoon sausage mixture into greased 2-quart casserole dish. Add zucchini to skillet; sauté for 5 minutes or until crisp-tender.

3. Combine tomato paste, water, basil and salt in medium bowl. Stir in rice. Spoon over sausage mixture. Arrange zucchini slices on top; sprinkle with mozzarella and Romano cheeses.

4. Cover. Bake in preheated 350°F oven for 20 minutes.   *Makes 6 servings*

Prep Time: 18 minutes
Cook Time: 20 minutes

*Adding 1 to 2 teaspoons of butter or oil to rice while
it cooks will help prevent it from boiling over.*

Beef

Athens Casserole

2 tablespoons vegetable oil
1½ pounds eggplant, peeled, cut crosswise into ¼-inch slices
1½ pounds ground beef
2 cups chopped onions
1 medium green bell pepper, cut into strips
1 medium yellow bell pepper, cut into strips
1 medium red bell pepper, cut into strips
¼ cup chopped fresh parsley
¼ cup dry red wine
1 teaspoon garlic powder
1 teaspoon ground cinnamon
Salt and black pepper
2 cans (28 ounces each) stewed tomatoes
8 ounces feta cheese, crumbled
4 eggs, beaten
½ cup bread crumbs

1. Preheat oven to 350°F.

2. Heat oil in large skillet over medium-high heat. Add eggplant and brown on both sides, 5 to 7 minutes; set aside on paper towels to drain.

3. In same skillet, cook and stir ground beef, onions and bell peppers over medium heat until beef is browned and onions are transparent. Add parsley, wine, garlic powder and cinnamon; mix well. Season with salt and black pepper.

4. Pour ⅓ of tomatoes into 13×9-inch baking dish. Layer with ⅓ of eggplant, ⅓ of beef mixture and ⅓ of cheese. Repeat layers twice. Pour eggs over top; sprinkle with bread crumbs.

5. Bake 45 minutes or until heated through and bubbly.   *Makes 10 servings*

Athens Casserole

Thai-Style Beef & Rice

1 (6.2-ounce) package RICE-A-RONI® Fried Rice
2 tablespoons margarine or butter
1 pound boneless sirloin or top round steak, cut into thin strips
2 cloves garlic, minced
¼ teaspoon crushed red pepper flakes
1 tablespoon sesame oil or vegetable oil
2 cups fresh or frozen snow peas, halved if large
½ cup red and/or yellow bell pepper strips
3 tablespoons soy sauce
1 tablespoon peanut butter
¼ cup chopped cilantro (optional)

1. In large skillet over medium heat, sauté rice-vermicelli mix with margarine until vermicelli is golden brown.

2. Slowly stir in 2 cups water and Special Seasonings; bring to a boil. Reduce heat to low. Cover; simmer 15 to 20 minutes or until rice is tender. Let stand 3 minutes.

3. Meanwhile, toss steak with garlic and red pepper flakes; set aside. In another large skillet or wok over medium-high heat, heat oil until hot. Add snow peas and bell pepper; stir-fry 2 minutes. Add meat mixture; stir-fry 2 minutes. Add soy sauce and peanut butter; stir-fry 1 minute or until meat is barely pink inside and vegetables are crisp-tender. Serve meat mixture over rice; sprinkle with cilantro, if desired. *Makes 4 servings*

Prep Time: 15 minutes
Cook Time: 30 minutes

Thai-Style Beef & Rice

Baked Black Bean Chili

1½ pounds ground beef
¼ cup chopped sweet onion
¼ cup chopped green bell pepper
1 can (15 ounces) black beans, rinsed and drained
1 can (14½ ounces) diced tomatoes with green chiles
1 can (14½ ounces) beef broth
1 can (8 ounces) tomato sauce
5 tablespoons chili powder
1 tablespoon sugar
1 tablespoon ground cumin
1 teaspoon dried minced onion
⅛ teaspoon garlic powder
⅛ teaspoon ground ginger
2 cups (8 ounces) shredded Mexican cheese blend

1. Preheat oven to 350°F. Cook and stir beef, onion and bell pepper in large skillet over medium-high heat until meat is no longer pink. Drain and transfer to 4-quart casserole.

2. Add remaining ingredients except cheese; stir until well blended. Cover and bake 30 minutes, stirring every 10 minutes. Uncover; top with cheese. Return to oven about 5 minutes or until cheese melts.   *Makes 6 to 8 servings*

Ground beef is a fairly meaningless term. Most people want to know what kind of beef has been ground. To meet USDA standards, all ground beef must be at least 70 percent lean. Ground sirloin and ground round are the leanest. Ground chuck contains more fat and therefore produces juicier hamburgers and meat loaf. If you are not sure what to buy, ask your butcher.

Baked Black Bean Chili

Contadina® Classic Lasagne

1 pound dry lasagne noodles, cooked
1 tablespoon olive or vegetable oil
1 cup chopped onion
½ cup chopped green bell pepper
2 cloves garlic, minced
1½ pounds lean ground beef
2 cans (14.5 ounces each) CONTADINA® Recipe Ready Diced Tomatoes, undrained
1 can (8 ounces) CONTADINA Tomato Sauce
1 can (6 ounces) CONTADINA Tomato Paste
½ cup dry red wine or beef broth
1½ teaspoons salt
1 teaspoon dried oregano leaves, crushed
1 teaspoon dried basil leaves, crushed
½ teaspoon ground black pepper
1 egg
1 cup (8 ounces) ricotta cheese
2 cups (8 ounces) shredded mozzarella cheese, divided

1. Cook pasta according to package directions; drain.

2. Meanwhile, heat oil in large skillet. Add onion, bell pepper and garlic; sauté for 3 minutes or until vegetables are tender.

3. Add beef; cook for 5 to 6 minutes or until evenly browned.

4. Add undrained tomatoes, tomato sauce, tomato paste, wine, salt, oregano, basil and black pepper; bring to a boil. Reduce heat to low; simmer, uncovered, for 20 minutes, stirring occasionally.

5. Beat egg slightly in medium bowl. Stir in ricotta cheese and 1 cup mozzarella cheese.

6. Layer one third of noodles, half of meat sauce, one third of noodles, all of ricotta cheese mixture, remaining noodles and remaining meat sauce in ungreased 13×9-inch baking dish. Sprinkle with remaining mozzarella cheese.

7. Bake in preheated 350°F oven for 25 to 30 minutes or until heated through. Let stand for 10 minutes before cutting to serve. *Makes 10 servings*

Prep Time: 35 minutes
Cook Time: 30 minutes
Stand Time: 10 minutes

Contadina® Classic Lasagne

Green Dragon Stir-Fry

2 tablespoons vegetable oil, divided
1 pound beef flank steak, very thinly sliced
1 bunch asparagus *or* 8 ounces green beans, cut into 2-inch pieces
1 green bell pepper, cut into strips
1 cup julienned carrots
3 large green onions, sliced
1 tablespoon minced fresh ginger
1 clove garlic, minced
¼ cup water
1 tablespoon soy sauce
1 tablespoon TABASCO® brand Green Pepper Sauce
½ teaspoon salt
2 cups hot cooked rice (optional)

Heat 1 tablespoon oil in 12-inch skillet over medium-high heat. Add flank steak; cook until well browned on all sides, stirring frequently. Remove steak to plate with slotted spoon.

Heat remaining 1 tablespoon oil in skillet over medium heat. Add asparagus, green bell pepper, carrots, green onions, ginger and garlic; cook about 3 minutes, stirring frequently. Add water, soy sauce, TABASCO® Green Pepper Sauce, salt and steak; heat to boiling over high heat.

Reduce heat to low; simmer, uncovered, 3 minutes, stirring occasionally. Serve with rice, if desired. *Makes 4 servings*

Note: This stir-fry is also delicious served over ramen or soba noodles.

Green Dragon Stir-Fry

Hearty Beef and Potato Casserole

1 package (about 17 ounces) refrigerated fully cooked beef pot roast in gravy*
3 cups frozen hash brown potatoes, divided
¼ teaspoon salt
¼ teaspoon black pepper
1 can (about 14 ounces) diced tomatoes, well drained
½ cup canned chipotle chile sauce
1 cup (4 ounces) shredded sharp Cheddar cheese

Fully cooked beef roast can be found in the refrigerated prepared meats section of the supermarket.

1. Preheat oven to 375°F. Grease 11×7-inch baking dish.

2. Drain and discard gravy from beef. Cut beef into ¼-inch-thick slices; set aside. Place 2 cups potatoes in prepared baking dish. Sprinkle with salt and pepper. Top with beef. Combine tomatoes and chipotle sauce in small bowl; spread evenly over beef. Top with remaining potatoes. Sprinkle with Cheddar cheese.

3. Lightly cover dish with foil. Bake 20 minutes. Remove foil; bake 20 minutes longer or until hot and bubbly. Let stand 5 to 10 minutes before serving.

Makes 6 servings

A mercury thermometer made for the oven is recommended for every kitchen. It allows the cook to read the actual oven temperature, which often varies from the dial setting. Remember that the oven temperature of a normal electric oven fluctuates continuously in a range as wide as 75°F. When checking the dial setting for accuracy, check the oven temperature on the thermometer frequently through the glass of the oven door if possible.

Tamale Beef Squares

1 (6½-ounce) package corn muffin and bread mix
⅓ cup milk
¼ cup egg substitute
1 tablespoon canola oil
1 pound ground beef
¾ cup chopped onion
1 cup frozen corn
1 can (about 14 ounces) Mexican-style stewed tomatoes, undrained
2 teaspoons cornstarch
¾ cup shredded sharp Cheddar cheese (3 ounces)

1. Preheat oven to 400°F. Spray 12×8-inch baking dish with nonstick cooking spray.

2. Place corn muffin mix, milk, egg substitute and oil in large bowl; stir until well blended. Spread in prepared dish.

3. Cook ground beef and onion in large skillet over medium-high heat until beef is lightly browned, stirring to break up meat; drain fat. Stir in corn.

4. Combine tomatoes with juice and cornstarch in medium bowl; stir until well blended, breaking up any large pieces of tomato. Stir into beef mixture. Bring to a boil, stirring frequently.

5. Spoon beef mixture over corn muffin batter. Cover with foil. Bake 15 minutes. Uncover; bake 10 minutes more. Sprinkle with cheese. Return to oven; bake 2 to 3 minutes or until cheese melts. Let stand 5 minutes. Cut into squares to serve.

Makes 6 servings

Tamale Beef Squares

Beef in Wine Sauce

4 pounds boneless beef chuck roast, cut into 1½- to 2-inch cubes
2 tablespoons garlic powder
2 cans (10¾ ounces each) condensed golden mushroom soup, undiluted
1 can (8 ounces) sliced mushrooms, drained
¾ cup dry sherry
1 envelope (about 1 ounce) dry onion soup mix
1 bag (20 ounces) frozen sliced carrots, thawed

Preheat oven to 325°F. Spray heavy 4-quart casserole or Dutch oven with nonstick cooking spray. Sprinkle beef with garlic powder. Place in prepared casserole. Combine canned soup, mushrooms, sherry and dry soup mix in medium bowl. Pour over meat; mix well. Cover; bake 3 hours or until meat is very tender. Add carrots during last 15 minutes of baking.

Makes 6 to 8 servings

Taco Pasta Casserole

8 ounces uncooked rotini pasta
1 pound ground beef
2 cloves garlic, minced
1 (15-ounce) can tomato sauce
⅔ cup whole kernel corn
⅓ cup diced red bell pepper
1 (1¼-ounce) package taco seasoning
2 tablespoons water
1 teaspoon dried oregano leaves
1 cup shredded cojack cheese, divided
½ cup reduced-fat sour cream

Cook pasta according to package directions; drain.

In large nonstick skillet, brown ground beef and garlic; drain thoroughly. Stir in tomato sauce, corn, bell pepper, taco seasoning, water and oregano. Bring to a boil; simmer 5 minutes.

Combine pasta, ½ cup cheese and sour cream. Spoon into 2-quart baking dish coated with nonstick cooking spray. Top with meat mixture and remaining ½ cup cheese. Bake uncovered at 350°F for 30 minutes. *Makes 6 servings*

*Favorite recipe from **North Dakota Wheat Commission***

Beef in Wine Sauce

Stir-Fried Orange Beef

  2 Florida oranges
1¼ pounds top round steak, trimmed
  ½ cup Florida orange juice, divided
  2 tablespoons low-sodium soy sauce
  1 tablespoon plus 1 teaspoon cornstarch, divided
  2 teaspoons brown sugar, divided
  ½ cup low-sodium chicken broth
  1 tablespoon dark sesame oil
  1 teaspoon finely minced fresh gingerroot
  1 clove garlic, minced
  4 cups broccoli flowerets
  4 medium scallions, cut into 2-inch pieces
  1 can (8 ounces) sliced water chestnuts, rinsed and drained
  3 tablespoons chopped fresh cilantro

Remove thin strips of rind from oranges with paring knife or zester; set aside. Section oranges; set aside. Cut steak along grain into 2-inch-wide strips. Cut steak across grain into ¼-inch-thick slices.

Combine steak, 2 tablespoons orange juice, soy sauce, 1 tablespoon cornstarch and 1 teaspoon brown sugar; stir to combine. Set aside.

Combine chicken broth, remaining 6 tablespoons orange juice, 1 teaspoon cornstarch and 1 teaspoon brown sugar in small bowl until well blended. Heat sesame oil in large nonstick skillet over medium-high heat until hot, but not smoking. Add reserved steak; stir-fry 3 to 4 minutes until steak is browned. Remove from skillet. Add ginger, garlic, reserved orange rind, broccoli, scallions, water chestnuts and chicken broth mixture. Stir-fry 2 to 3 minutes until vegetables begin to soften. Add cilantro and reserved steak (with juices); cook and stir until sauce has thickened slightly. Stir in orange sections and serve immediately. *Makes 6 servings*

Favorite recipe from **Florida Department of Citrus**

Old-Fashioned Beef Pot Pie

1 pound ground beef
1 can (11 ounces) condensed beef with vegetables and barley soup, undiluted
½ cup water
1 package (10 ounces) frozen peas and carrots, thawed and drained
½ teaspoon seasoned salt
⅛ teaspoon garlic powder
⅛ teaspoon ground black pepper
1 cup (4 ounces) shredded Cheddar cheese, divided
1⅓ cups *French's*® French Fried Onions, divided
1 package (7½ ounces) refrigerated biscuits

Preheat oven to 350°F. In large skillet, brown ground beef in large chunks; drain. Stir in soup, water, vegetables and seasonings; bring to a boil. Reduce heat and simmer, uncovered, 5 minutes. Remove from heat; stir in ½ cup cheese and ⅔ *cup* French Fried Onions.

Pour mixture into 12×8-inch baking dish. Cut each biscuit in half; place, cut side down, around edge of casserole. Bake, uncovered, 15 to 20 minutes or until biscuits are done. Top with remaining cheese and ⅔ *cup* onions; bake, uncovered, 5 minutes or until onions are golden brown.

Makes 4 to 6 servings

*Pot pies are among the glories of country cooking. American in origin,
they consist of chunks of cooked meat and vegetables enveloped in a sauce,
placed in a deep dish or pie pan and covered with a blanket of flaky pastry.
The term pot pie first appeared in American print as early as 1792.*

Mexican Lasagna

1 jar (1 pound 10 ounces) RAGÚ® Old World Style® Pasta Sauce, divided
1 pound ground beef
1 can (15¼ ounces) whole kernel corn, drained
4½ teaspoons chili powder
6 (8½-inch) flour tortillas
2 cups shredded Cheddar cheese (about 8 ounces)

1. Preheat oven to 350°F. Reserve 1 cup Ragú Pasta Sauce. In 10-inch skillet, brown ground beef over medium-high heat; drain. Stir in remaining Ragú Pasta Sauce, corn and chili powder.

2. In 13×9-inch baking dish, spread 1 cup beef mixture; top with two tortillas, overlapping edges slightly. Layer half the beef mixture and one third of the cheese over tortillas; repeat layers, ending with tortillas. Spread tortillas with reserved pasta sauce.

3. Bake 30 minutes. Top with remaining cheese and bake an additional 10 minutes or until sauce is bubbling and cheese is melted.

Makes 8 servings

Prep Time: 10 minutes
Cook Time: 40 minutes

Tip: Substitute refried beans for ground beef for a meatless main dish.

Chili powder is a spice blend typically made up of ground dried chiles, cloves, coriander, cumin, garlic and oregano.

Mexican Lasagna

String Pie

   1 pound ground beef
   ½ cup chopped onion
   ¼ cup chopped green bell pepper
   1 jar (15½ ounces) spaghetti sauce
   8 ounces spaghetti, cooked and drained
   ⅓ cup grated Parmesan cheese
   2 eggs, beaten
   2 teaspoons butter, melted
   1 cup cottage cheese
   ½ cup (2 ounces) shredded mozzarella cheese

Preheat oven to 350°F. Cook beef, onion and green pepper in large skillet over medium-high heat until meat is browned. Drain fat. Stir in spaghetti sauce. Combine spaghetti, Parmesan cheese, eggs and melted butter in large bowl; mix well. Place in 13×9-inch baking pan. Spread cottage cheese over top; cover with sauce mixture. Sprinkle with mozzarella cheese. Bake until mixture is thoroughly heated and cheese is melted, about 20 minutes.

Makes 6 to 8 servings

Favorite recipe from **North Dakota Beef Commission**

Beef Stroganoff

   12 ounces uncooked wide egg noodles
   1 can (10¾ ounces) condensed cream of mushroom soup, undiluted
   1 cup (8 ounces) sour cream
   1 package (1¼ ounces) dry onion soup mix
   1½ pounds ground beef
   1 cup frozen peas, thawed

1. Place 3 quarts water in 8-quart stockpot; bring to a boil over high heat. Stir in noodles; boil, uncovered, 6 minutes or until tender. Drain.

2. Meanwhile, combine mushroom soup, sour cream and onion soup mix in medium bowl. Stir until blended; set aside. Brown meat in large skillet over high heat 6 to 8 minutes or until meat is no longer pink, stirring to separate meat. Pour off drippings. Reduce heat to low. Add soup mixture; stir over low heat until bubbly. Stir in peas; heat through. Serve over noodles.

Makes 6 servings

String Pie

Beef & Broccoli Pepper Steak

3 tablespoons margarine or butter, divided
1 pound sirloin or top round steak, cut into thin strips
1 (6.8-ounce) package RICE-A-RONI® Beef Flavor
2 cups broccoli flowerets
½ cup red or green bell pepper strips
1 small onion, thinly sliced

1. In large skillet over medium-high heat, melt 1 tablespoon margarine. Add steak; sauté 3 minutes or until just browned. Remove from skillet; set aside.

2. In same skillet over medium heat, sauté rice-vermicelli mix with remaining 2 tablespoons margarine until vermicelli is golden brown. Slowly stir in 2½ cups water and Special Seasonings; bring to a boil. Reduce heat to low. Cover; simmer 10 minutes.

3. Stir in steak, broccoli, bell pepper and onion; return to a simmer. Cover; simmer 5 to 10 minutes or until rice is tender.   *Makes 4 servings*

Prep Time: 10 minutes
Cook Time: 30 minutes

Rainbow Casserole

5 potatoes, peeled and cut into thin slices
1 pound ground beef
1 onion, peeled, halved, then cut into thin slices
   Salt and black pepper
1 can (about 28 ounces) stewed tomatoes, drained, juice reserved
1 cup frozen peas *or* 1 can (about 6 ounces) peas, drained

1. Preheat oven to 350°F. Spray 3-quart casserole with nonstick cooking spray.

2. Boil potatoes in salted water in large saucepan until almost tender. Drain. Meanwhile, cook ground beef in medium skillet over medium heat until no longer pink, stirring to separate meat. Drain and discard fat.

3. Layer half of ground beef, half of potatoes, half of onion, salt, pepper, half of tomatoes and half of peas. Repeat layers. Add reserved tomato juice.

4. Bake, covered, about 40 minutes or until most of liquid is absorbed.
Makes 4 to 6 servings

Beef & Broccoli Pepper Steak

It's a Keeper Casserole

1 tablespoon vegetable oil
½ cup chopped onion
¼ cup chopped green bell pepper
1 clove garlic, minced
2 tablespoons all-purpose flour
1 teaspoon sugar
½ teaspoon salt
½ teaspoon dried basil
½ teaspoon black pepper
1 can (about 16 ounces) whole tomatoes, cut up and drained
1 package (about 16 ounces) frozen meatballs, cooked
1½ cups cooked vegetables (any combination)
1 teaspoon beef bouillon granules
1 teaspoon Worcestershire sauce
1 can refrigerated buttermilk biscuits

1. Preheat oven to 400°F. Heat oil in large saucepan. Cook and stir onion, bell pepper and garlic over medium heat until vegetables are tender.

2. Stir in flour, sugar, salt, basil and black pepper. Slowly blend in tomatoes, meatballs, vegetables, bouillon and Worcestershire sauce. Cook and stir until slightly thickened and bubbling; pour into 2-quart casserole.

3. Unroll biscuits; place on top of casserole. Bake, uncovered, 15 minutes or until biscuits are golden. *Makes 4 servings*

It's a Keeper Casserole

Shepherd's Pie

1⅓ cups instant mashed potato flakes
1⅔ cups milk
2 tablespoons butter
1 teaspoon salt, divided
1 pound ground beef
¼ teaspoon black pepper
1 jar (12 ounces) beef gravy
1 package (10 ounces) frozen mixed vegetables, thawed and drained
¾ cup grated Parmesan cheese

1. Preheat broiler. Prepare 4 servings of mashed potatoes according to package directions, using milk, butter and ½ teaspoon salt.

2. While mashed potatoes are cooking, brown beef in medium broiler-proof skillet over medium-high heat, stirring to separate. Drain drippings. Sprinkle beef with remaining ½ teaspoon salt and pepper. Add gravy and vegetables; mix well. Cook over medium-low heat 5 minutes or until hot.

3. Spoon prepared potatoes around outside edge of skillet, leaving 3-inch circle in center. Sprinkle cheese evenly over potatoes. Broil 4 to 5 inches from heat 3 minutes or until cheese is golden brown and beef mixture is bubbly.

Makes 4 servings

Prep and Cook Time: 28 minutes

Use a rotary cheese grater to make quick work of grating hard cheeses such as Parmesan. This hand-held utensil consists of a food container with a grating cylinder and a hand-turned crank. Hard cheeses can also be grated on a box grater or flat metal grater with small holes.

Shepherd's Pie

Spicy Quick and Easy Chili

    1 pound ground beef
    1 large clove garlic, minced
    1 can (15¼ ounces) DEL MONTE® Whole Kernel Golden Sweet Corn,
        drained
    1 can (16 ounces) kidney beans, drained
 1½ cups salsa (mild, medium or hot)
    1 can (4 ounces) diced green chiles, undrained

1. Brown meat with garlic in large saucepan; drain.

2. Add remaining ingredients. Simmer, uncovered, 10 minutes, stirring occasionally. Sprinkle with chopped green onions, if desired.

Makes 4 servings

Prep and Cook Time: 15 minutes

Nifty Nacho Dinner

    8 ounces lean ground beef
    1 (6.8-ounce) package RICE-A-RONI® Beef Flavor
    2 tablespoons margarine or butter
    1 (16-ounce) can refried beans
    1 (11-ounce) can Mexican-style corn or sweet corn, drained
 1½ cups (6 ounces) shredded Cheddar cheese, divided
    Tortilla chips

1. In large skillet over medium-high heat, brown ground beef. Remove from skillet; drain. Set aside.

2. In same skillet over medium heat, sauté rice-vermicelli mix with margarine until vermicelli is golden brown.

3. Slowly stir in 2½ cups water and Special Seasonings; bring to a boil. Reduce heat to low. Cover; simmer 10 minutes.

4. Stir in refried beans, corn, 1 cup cheese and beef; return to a simmer. Cover; simmer 5 to 10 minutes or until rice is tender. Top with remaining ½ cup cheese. Serve in skillet with tortilla chips.

Makes 6 servings

Prep Time: 5 minutes
Cook Time: 30 minutes

Spicy Quick and Easy Chili

Meat Crust Pie

   1 pound ground beef
   2 cans (8 ounces each) tomato sauce, divided
   ½ cup seasoned dry bread crumbs
   ½ cup chopped green bell pepper, divided
   ¼ cup minced onion
   1 teaspoon salt, divided
   ⅛ teaspoon dried oregano
   ⅛ teaspoon black pepper
   1 cup water
1⅓ cups uncooked instant rice
   1 cup (4 ounces) shredded Cheddar cheese, divided

1. Preheat oven to 350°F. Combine beef, ½ cup tomato sauce, bread crumbs, ¼ cup bell pepper, onion, ½ teaspoon salt, oregano and black pepper in large bowl; mix well. Pat onto bottom and up side of ungreased 9-inch deep-dish pie plate.

2. Bring water and remaining ½ teaspoon salt to a boil in medium saucepan. Stir in rice; cover and remove from heat. Let stand 5 minutes or until water is absorbed. Add remaining 1½ cups tomato sauce, ½ cup cheese and remaining ¼ cup bell pepper to rice; mix well. Spoon rice mixture into meat shell. Cover with foil; bake 25 minutes.

3. Remove from oven; drain fat carefully, holding pan lid over pie to keep it from sliding. Top with remaining ½ cup cheese. Bake, uncovered, 10 to 15 minutes or until cheese melts. Carefully drain fat again. Garnish as desired. Cut into wedges to serve. *Makes 6 to 8 servings*

Meat Crust Pie

Beef Teriyaki Stir-Fry

1 cup uncooked rice
1 boneless beef top sirloin steak (about 1 pound)
½ cup teriyaki marinade and sauce, divided
2 tablespoons vegetable oil, divided
1 medium onion, halved and sliced
2 cups frozen green beans, rinsed and drained

1. Cook rice according to package directions, omitting salt.

2. Cut beef lengthwise in half, then crosswise into ⅛-inch slices. Combine beef and ¼ cup marinade in medium bowl; set aside.

3. Heat 1½ teaspoons oil in wok or large skillet over medium-high heat until hot. Add onion; stir-fry 3 to 4 minutes or until crisp-tender. Remove from wok to medium bowl.

4. Heat 1½ teaspoons oil in wok. Stir-fry beans 3 minutes or until crisp-tender and hot. Drain off excess liquid. Add beans to onions in bowl.

5. Heat remaining 1 tablespoon oil in wok. Drain beef, discarding marinade. Stir-fry half of beef 2 minutes or until barely pink in center. Remove to bowl. Repeat with remaining beef. Return beef and accumulated juices in bowl to wok. Stir in vegetables and remaining ¼ cup marinade; cook and stir 1 minute or until heated through. Serve with rice. *Makes 4 servings*

Prep and Cook Time: 22 minutes

With regards to food safety and cutting boards, there is no definitive answer as to what material is safest for use with foods that may contain bacteria, such as poultry and meat. No matter what the material, it must always be thoroughly washed in hot, soapy water after it comes in contact with poultry or meat and before it is used with any other foods.

Beef Teriyaki Stir-Fry

Stuffed Mexican Pizza Pie

1 pound ground beef
1 large onion, chopped
1 large green bell pepper, chopped
1½ cups UNCLE BEN'S® Instant Rice
2 cans (14½ ounces each) Mexican-style stewed tomatoes, undrained
⅔ cup water
2 cups (8 ounces) shredded Mexican-style seasoned Monterey Jack-Colby cheese blend, divided
1 package (10 ounces) refrigerated pizza crust dough

1. Preheat oven to 425°F. Spray 13×9-inch baking pan with cooking spray; set aside.

2. Spray large nonstick skillet with nonstick cooking spray; heat over high heat until hot. Add beef, onion and bell pepper; cook and stir 5 minutes or until meat is no longer pink.

3. Add rice, stewed tomatoes and water. Bring to a boil. Pour beef mixture into prepared baking pan. Sprinkle with 1¼ cups cheese and stir until blended.

4. Unroll pizza crust dough on work surface. Place dough in one even layer over mixture in baking pan. Cut 6 to 8 slits in dough with sharp knife. Bake 10 minutes or until crust is lightly browned. Sprinkle top of crust with remaining ¾ cup cheese; continue baking 4 minutes or until cheese is melted and crust is deep golden brown.

5. Let stand 5 minutes before cutting.   *Makes 6 servings*

Mini Meat Loaves & Vegetables

1½ pounds lean ground beef
1 egg
1 can (8 ounces) tomato sauce, divided
1⅓ cups *French's*® French Fried Onions, divided
½ teaspoon salt
½ teaspoon Italian seasoning
6 small red potatoes, thinly sliced (about 1½ cups)
1 bag (16 ounces) frozen vegetable combination (broccoli, corn, red bell pepper), thawed and drained
Salt
Black pepper

Preheat oven to 375°F. In medium bowl, combine ground beef, egg, ½ *can* tomato sauce, ⅔ *cup* French Fried Onions, ½ teaspoon salt and Italian seasoning. Shape into 3 mini loaves and place in 13×9-inch baking dish. Arrange potatoes around loaves. Bake, covered, at 375°F for 35 minutes. Spoon vegetables around meat loaves; stir to combine with potatoes. Lightly season vegetables with salt and pepper, if desired. Top meat loaves with remaining tomato sauce. Bake, uncovered, 15 minutes or until meat loaves are done. Top loaves with remaining ⅔ *cup* onions; bake, uncovered, 3 minutes or until onions are golden brown. *Makes 6 servings*

Microwave Directions: Prepare meat loaves as above. Arrange potatoes on bottom of 12×8-inch microwave-safe dish; place meat loaves on potatoes. Cook, covered, on HIGH 13 minutes. Rotate dish halfway through cooking time. Add vegetables and season as above. Top meat loaves with remaining tomato sauce. Cook, covered, 7 minutes or until meat loaves are done. Rotate dish halfway through cooking time. Top loaves with remaining ⅔ *cup* onions; cook, uncovered, 1 minute. Let stand 5 minutes.

Tortilla Beef Casserole

1 package (about 17 ounces) refrigerated fully cooked beef pot roast in gravy
6 (6-inch) corn tortillas, cut into 1-inch pieces
1 jar (16 ounces) salsa
1½ cups frozen corn
1 cup black or pinto beans, rinsed and drained
1 cup (8 ounces) Mexican cheese blend

Fully cooked beef roast can be found in the refrigerated prepared meats section of the supermarket.

1. Preheat oven to 350°F. Lightly spray 11×7-inch or 2-quart casserole with nonstick cooking spray.

2. Drain and discard gravy from beef; cut or shred beef into bite-size pieces.

3. Combine beef, tortillas, salsa, corn and beans in large bowl; mix well. Transfer to prepared casserole. Bake 20 minutes or until heated through. Top with cheese; bake 5 minutes more or until cheese is melted.

Makes 4 servings

Wild Rice Beefy Vegetable Casserole

1 pound lean ground beef
1 cup chopped onion
1 pound frozen broccoli, carrots & cauliflower blend, thawed and drained
1 can (10¾ ounces) condensed cream of celery soup, undiluted
1 can (8 ounces) tomato sauce
3 cups cooked wild rice
2 cups shredded mild Cheddar cheese, divided
2 teaspoons dried Italian seasoning
1 teaspoon salt
½ teaspoon black pepper

Preheat oven to 350°F. In large skillet, brown beef and onion; drain. Add vegetables, soup, tomato sauce, wild rice, 1½ cups cheese and seasonings; mix lightly. Place in 3-quart casserole; top with remaining ½ cup cheese. Cover; bake 25 to 30 minutes or until heated through. Uncover; bake 5 minutes.

Makes 6 to 8 servings

Favorite recipe from **Minnesota Cultivated Wild Rice Council**

Tortilla Beef Casserole

Easy Vegetable Beef Stew

1 pound beef for stew, cut into 1-inch pieces
1 can (14½ ounces) diced tomatoes, undrained
1 medium onion, cut into 8 wedges
4 carrots, cut into 1-inch pieces
1 green or red bell pepper, diced
1 stalk celery, sliced
1 teaspoon dried Italian seasoning
½ teaspoon salt
½ teaspoon black pepper
1 tablespoon vegetable oil
1 package (8 ounces) sliced mushrooms

1. Preheat oven to 325°F.

2. Combine beef, tomatoes with juice and onion in Dutch oven. Cover tightly; bake 1 hour.

3. Add carrots, bell pepper, celery, Italian seasoning, salt and black pepper to beef mixture; stir. Cover; bake 45 minutes or until beef and carrots are tender.

4. Heat oil in large skillet over medium heat. Add mushrooms; cook and stir 10 minutes or until lightly browned and tender. Stir mushrooms into stew. Adjust seasonings to taste.   *Makes 4 servings*

Variation: Two unpeeled medium red potatoes, cut into 2-inch pieces, can be added with carrots.

A Dutch oven is a large, heavy covered pot with two short handles. It is used for the slow, moist cooking of a large quantity of food. It is ideal for soups and stews and for braising large pieces of meat. Choose one with ovenproof handles if you would like the convenience of using it in the oven as well as on the rangetop. Dutch ovens range in size from 5 to 8 quarts. Larger pots are generally referred to as stockpots.

Easy Vegetable Beef Stew

Chili & Potato Casserole

1 pound HILLSHIRE FARM® Yard-O-Beef, cut into small cubes
1 cup chopped yellow onion
1 egg, lightly beaten
¼ cup bread crumbs
1 tablespoon chili powder
   Salt to taste
3 cups prepared mashed potatoes
1 can (11 ounces) succotash, drained
¼ cup thinly sliced green onions
1 cup (4 ounces) shredded taco-flavored cheese

Preheat oven to 375°F.

Combine Yard-O-Beef, yellow onion, egg, bread crumbs, chili powder and salt in large bowl; mix thoroughly. Pour beef mixture into medium baking dish, pressing mixture firmly onto bottom of dish. Bake 20 minutes. Pour off any juices.

Mix potatoes, succotash and green onions in medium bowl. Spread potato mixture over beef mixture; sprinkle with cheese. Broil 3 to 4 inches from heat source 3 to 5 minutes or until top is lightly browned.   *Makes 4 to 6 servings*

Tip: Frozen casseroles should be reheated in a 350°F oven. Add some liquid during cooking if the food seems dry.

Succotash is a popular dish in the Southern United States. It is traditionally a combination of corn, lima beans and sometimes green or red bell pepper.

Chili & Potato Casserole

Steak Stir-Fry

1 beef top sirloin steak (about 1½ pounds)
1 package (8 ounces) dry rice stick noodles
¼ cup dry white wine
¼ cup soy sauce
1 tablespoon plus 1½ teaspoons cornstarch
1 tablespoon sugar
2 teaspoons finely chopped fresh ginger
2 tablespoons vegetable oil
2 teaspoons minced garlic
2 cups sliced mushrooms
2 cups matchstick-size carrot sticks
1 cup green bell pepper strips
½ cup sliced green onions
4 cups fresh spinach leaves, washed and drained

1. Cut beef lengthwise in half, then crosswise into ¼-inch strips. Set aside. Cook noodles according to package directions. Drain well. Set aside.

2. While noodles are cooking, combine wine, soy sauce, cornstarch, sugar and ginger in medium bowl; whisk to blend. Add beef strips; toss to coat well. Set aside.

3. Heat oil and garlic in large nonstick skillet or wok over high heat. Add mushrooms, carrots, bell peppers and green onions; stir-fry 4 minutes. Transfer vegetables to bowl. Cover; keep warm.

4. Add beef strips and marinade to wok; stir-fry 6 minutes. Return vegetables to skillet; stir until blended.

5. Line serving platter with spinach. Arrange noodles over spinach; top with beef mixture. Serve immediately. *Makes 4 servings*

Prep and Cook Time: 20 minutes

Tip: Stir-fry meat can be purchased presliced from the supermarket meat case.

Steak Stir-Fry

Taco Pot Pie

1 pound ground beef
1 package (1¼ ounces) taco seasoning mix
¼ cup water
1 can (8 ounces) kidney beans, rinsed and drained
1 cup chopped tomato
¾ cup frozen corn, thawed
¾ cup frozen peas, thawed
1½ cups (6 ounces) shredded Cheddar cheese
1 can (11½ ounces) refrigerated corn breadstick dough

1. Preheat oven to 400°F. Brown meat in medium ovenproof skillet over medium-high heat, stirring to separate; drain drippings. Add seasoning mix and water to skillet. Cook over medium-low heat 3 minutes or until most of liquid is absorbed, stirring occasionally.

2. Stir in beans, tomato, corn and peas. Cook 3 minutes or until mixture is hot. Remove from heat; stir in cheese.

3. Unwrap breadstick dough; separate into 16 strips. Twist strips, cutting to fit skillet. Arrange attractively over meat mixture. Press ends of dough lightly to edge of skillet to secure. Bake 15 minutes or until corn bread is golden brown and meat mixture is bubbly.

Makes 4 to 6 servings

Prep and Cook Time: 30 minutes

Fresh tomatoes should never be refrigerated before cutting because cold temperatures cause their flesh to become mealy and lose flavor. Store them at room temperature. Ripening can be hastened by placing them in a paper bag.

Taco Pot Pie

Stir-Fry Tomato Beef

1 cup uncooked long-grain white rice
1 pound flank steak
1 tablespoon cornstarch
1 tablespoon soy sauce
2 cloves garlic, minced
1 teaspoon minced gingerroot *or* ¼ teaspoon ground ginger
1 tablespoon vegetable oil
1 can (14½ ounces) DEL MONTE® Stewed Tomatoes - Seasoned with
    Onions, Celery & Green Peppers

1. Cook rice according to package directions.

2. Meanwhile, cut meat in half lengthwise, then cut crosswise into thin slices.

3. Combine cornstarch, soy sauce, garlic and ginger in medium bowl. Add meat; toss to coat.

4. Heat oil in large skillet over high heat. Add meat; cook, stirring constantly, until browned. Add undrained tomatoes; cook until thickened, about 5 minutes, stirring frequently.

5. Serve meat mixture over hot cooked rice. Garnish, if desired.

Makes 4 to 6 servings

Prep Time: 10 minutes
Cook Time: 20 minutes

White rice has been polished to remove the husk, bran and germ. Vitamins and minerals are then added to most white rice to replace the nutrients lost in the milling process. It is available in short-, medium- and long-grain grades. Instant or quick-cooking rice has been fully or partially cooked before being dehydrated and packaged. It only takes a few minutes to prepare but does not have the same texture or flavor as polished white rice.

Stir-Fry Tomato Beef

Patchwork Casserole

2 pounds ground beef
2 cups chopped green bell peppers
1 cup chopped onions
2 pounds frozen Southern-style hash-brown potatoes, thawed
2 cans (8 ounces each) tomato sauce
1 cup water
1 can (6 ounces) tomato paste
1 teaspoon salt
½ teaspoon dried basil
¼ teaspoon black pepper
1 pound pasteurized process American cheese, thinly sliced and divided

1. Preheat oven to 350°F.

2. Brown beef in large skillet over medium heat about 10 minutes; drain fat. Add bell peppers and onions; cook and stir about 4 minutes or until tender. Stir in potatoes, tomato sauce, water, tomato paste, salt, basil and black pepper.

3. Spoon half of mixture into 13×9-inch baking pan or 3-quart baking dish; top with half of cheese. Spoon remaining beef mixture evenly on top of cheese. Cover pan with aluminum foil. Bake 45 minutes.

4. Cut remaining cheese into decorative shapes; place on top of casserole. Let stand loosely covered until cheese melts, about 5 minutes.

Makes 8 to 10 servings

Patchwork Casserole

Lickety-Split Paella Pronto

1 tablespoon olive oil
1 large onion, chopped
2 cloves garlic, minced
1 jar (16 ounces) salsa
1 can (14½ ounces) diced tomatoes, undrained
1 can (14 ounces) artichoke hearts, drained and quartered
1 can (14 ounces) chicken broth
1 package (about 8 ounces) uncooked yellow rice
1 can (12 ounces) solid white tuna, drained and flaked
1 package (9 to 10 ounces) frozen green peas
2 tablespoons finely chopped green onions (optional)
2 tablespoons finely chopped red bell pepper (optional)

1. Heat oil in large nonstick skillet over medium heat until hot. Add onion and garlic; cook and stir about 5 minutes or until onion is tender.

2. Stir in salsa, tomatoes with juice, artichokes, broth and rice. Bring to a boil. Cover; reduce heat to low and simmer 15 minutes.

3. Stir in tuna and peas. Cover; cook 5 to 10 minutes or until rice is tender and tuna and peas are heated through. Sprinkle each serving with green onions and red bell pepper, if desired.
Makes 4 to 6 servings

Lickety-Split Paella Pronto

243

Seafood & Vegetable Stir-Fry

    2 teaspoons olive oil
    ½ medium red or yellow bell pepper, cut into strips
    ½ medium onion, cut into wedges
   10 snow peas, trimmed and cut diagonally into halves
    1 clove garlic, minced
    6 ounces frozen cooked medium shrimp, thawed
    2 tablespoons stir-fry sauce
    1 cup hot cooked rice

1. Heat oil in large nonstick skillet over medium-high heat. Add vegetables; stir-fry 4 minutes. Add garlic; stir-fry 1 minute or until vegetables are crisp-tender.

2. Add shrimp and stir-fry sauce. Stir-fry 1 to 2 minutes or until hot. Serve over rice. *Makes 2 servings*

Fast Catfish in Foil

    4 catfish fillets (4 ounces each)
    2 cups shredded carrots
    6 ounces green beans, ends trimmed (about 60 beans)
    8 unpeeled baby red potatoes, unpeeled and quartered
      Nonstick cooking spray
    4 teaspoons lemon juice
    2 teaspoons dried parsley flakes
    1 teaspoon black pepper

1. Preheat oven to 425°F. Place one fillet, skin side down, on each of four 12×12-inch sheets of aluminum foil. Top each fillet with ½ cup shredded carrots, 15 green beans and 8 potato quarters.

2. Spray ingredients on each foil square with cooking spray. Sprinkle with 1 teaspoon lemon juice, ¼ teaspoon (or to taste) pepper and ½ teaspoon parsley flakes.

3. Fold foil squares into packets, sealing securely. Place packets on baking sheet; bake 30 minutes.

4. Remove packets from oven; let stand 5 minutes. Carefully open packets allowing steam to escape. Serve immediately. *Makes 4 servings*

Seafood & Vegetable Stir-Fry

Tuna and Caponata Sauce

Olive oil
2 cups diced, peeled eggplant
½ cup chopped onion
½ cup chopped celery
½ cup coarsely grated carrot
¼ pound mushrooms, chopped
1 can (14½ ounces) Italian pasta-style tomatoes*
1 (7-ounce) STARKIST Flavor Fresh Pouch® Tuna (Albacore or Chunk Light)
Salt and black pepper to taste
Hot cooked pasta

Or substitute 1 can (14½ ounces) cut-up tomatoes, ½ teaspoon minced or pressed garlic and 1 teaspoon Italian herb seasoning.

In 3-quart saucepan, heat several tablespoons olive oil over medium-high heat; sauté one third of eggplant until browned. Remove from pan; set aside. Repeat until all eggplant is browned and reserved. Heat several tablespoons oil; sauté onion, celery, carrot and mushrooms until onion is tender. Return eggplant to saucepan; stir in tomatoes and tuna. Simmer about 15 minutes; add salt and pepper. Serve over pasta.   *Makes 4 servings*

Prep Time: 25 minutes

Note: This recipe is easily doubled.

Caponata is a traditional Sicilian dish served as a salad, side dish or relish. It usually includes eggplant, onion, tomato and seasonings.

Tuna and Caponata Sauce

Salmon Casserole

    2 tablespoons butter
    2 cups sliced mushrooms
1½ cups chopped carrots
    1 cup frozen peas
    1 cup chopped celery
 ½ cup chopped onion
 ½ cup chopped red bell pepper
    1 tablespoon chopped fresh parsley
    1 clove garlic, minced
    1 teaspoon salt
 ½ teaspoon black pepper
 ½ teaspoon dried basil
    4 cups cooked rice
    1 can (14 ounces) red salmon, drained and flaked
    1 can (10¾ ounces) condensed cream of mushroom soup, undiluted
    2 cups (8 ounces) grated Cheddar or American cheese
 ½ cup sliced black olives

1. Preheat oven to 350°F. Spray 2-quart casserole with nonstick cooking spray; set aside.

2. Melt butter in large skillet or Dutch oven over medium heat. Add mushrooms, carrots, peas, celery, onion, bell pepper, parsley, garlic, salt, black pepper and basil; cook and stir 10 minutes or until vegetables are tender. Add rice, salmon, soup and cheese; mix well.

3. Transfer to prepared casserole; sprinkle with olives. Bake 30 minutes or until hot and bubbly. *Makes 8 servings*

Salmon Casserole

Zesty Seafood Lasagna

2 packages (1.8 ounces each) white sauce mix
4½ cups milk
1 teaspoon dried basil leaves
½ teaspoon dried thyme leaves
½ teaspoon garlic powder
¾ cup grated Parmesan cheese, divided
3 tablespoons *Frank's® RedHot®* Original Cayenne Pepper Sauce
9 oven-ready lasagna pasta sheets
2 packages (10 ounces each) frozen chopped spinach, thawed and
   squeezed
½ pound cooked shrimp
½ pound raw bay scallops or flaked imitation crabmeat
2 cups (8 ounces) shredded mozzarella cheese, divided

1. Preheat oven to 400°F. Prepare white sauce according to package directions using milk and adding basil, thyme and garlic powder in large saucepan. Stir in ½ cup Parmesan cheese and *Frank's RedHot* Sauce.

2. Spread 1 cup sauce on bottom of greased 13×9×2-inch casserole. Layer 3 pasta sheets crosswise over sauce. (Do not let edges touch.) Layer half of the spinach and seafood over pasta. Spoon 1 cup sauce over seafood; sprinkle with ¾ cup mozzarella cheese. Repeat layers a second time. Top with final layer of pasta sheets, remaining sauce and both cheeses.

3. Cover pan with greased foil. Bake 40 minutes. Remove foil; bake 10 minutes or until top is browned and pasta is fully cooked. Let stand 15 minutes before serving.   *Makes 8 servings*

Prep Time: 30 minutes
Cook Time: 50 minutes

Tip: Splash *Frank's RedHot* Sauce on foods after cooking instead of salt and black pepper. *Frank's RedHot* Sauce perks up the flavor of all foods!

Zesty Seafood Lasagna

Shrimp Primavera Pot Pie

1 can (10¾ ounces) condensed cream of shrimp soup, undiluted
1 package (12 ounces) frozen peeled medium raw shrimp
2 packages (1 pound each) frozen mixed vegetables, such as green beans, potatoes, onions and red bell peppers, thawed and drained
1 teaspoon dried dill weed
¼ teaspoon salt
¼ teaspoon black pepper
1 can (11 ounces) refrigerated breadstick dough

1. Preheat oven to 400°F. Heat soup in medium ovenproof skillet over medium-high heat 1 minute. Add shrimp; cook and stir 3 minutes or until shrimp begin to thaw. Stir in vegetables, dill, salt and pepper; mix well. Reduce heat to medium-low; cook and stir 3 minutes.

2. Unwrap breadstick dough; separate into 8 strips. Twist strips and arrange attractively over shrimp mixture in crisscross pattern, cutting to fit skillet. Press ends of dough lightly to edges of skillet to secure. Bake 18 minutes or until crust is golden brown and shrimp mixture is bubbly.   *Makes 4 to 6 servings*

Prep and Cook Time: 30 minutes

Crunchy Veg•All® Tuna Casserole

2 cups medium egg noodles
1 can (15 ounces) VEG•ALL® Original Mixed Vegetables, drained
1 can (12 ounces) solid white tuna in water, drained
1 can (10.75 ounces) condensed cream of celery soup, undiluted
1¼ cups whole milk
½ cup sour cream
1 tablespoon chopped fresh dill
1 cup crushed sour cream & onion potato chips

Combine all ingredients except potato chips in greased 1½-quart casserole dish.

Microwave, uncovered, on High for 10 to 12 minutes or until very thick. Let cool for 10 minutes.

Top with crushed potato chips and serve.   *Makes 4 to 6 servings*

Shrimp Primavera Pot Pie

Creamy Salmon with Green Beans

1 large salmon fillet (about ¾ pound)
2 tablespoons butter
1 large ripe tomato, cut into ½-inch pieces
1 small onion, coarsely chopped
2 tablespoons all-purpose flour
1 cup vegetable or chicken broth
1 package (9 ounces) frozen cut green beans, partially thawed
1 cup half-and-half
¼ teaspoon salt
¼ teaspoon white pepper
5 tablespoons grated Parmesan cheese, divided
    Hot cooked angel hair pasta

1. Rinse salmon and pat dry with paper towels. Remove skin and bones; discard. Cut salmon into ¾-inch pieces.

2. Heat wok over medium-high heat 1 minute or until hot. Add butter. Swirl to coat bottom; heat 30 seconds. Add salmon; stir-fry gently 3 to 4 minutes or until fish flakes easily when tested with fork. Remove to large bowl; cover and keep warm.

3. Add tomato and onion to wok; stir-fry about 5 minutes or until onion is tender. Stir in flour until well mixed. Increase heat to high. Stir in broth and beans; cook until sauce boils and thickens. Add salmon, half-and-half, salt and pepper; cook until heated through. Add half of cheese; toss until well mixed. Spoon salmon mixture over angel hair pasta. Sprinkle with remaining cheese. Garnish as desired. *Makes 4 servings*

Although salmon has a higher fat content than most fish, it is still very nutritious. Salmon's fat content is made up primarily of omega-3 fatty acids. There is a wealth of research available today that links consumption of omega-3 fatty acids with the reduced risk of heart attack and heart disease.

Creamy Salmon with Green Beans

Seafood Stew

2 tablespoons butter
1 cup chopped onion
1 cup green bell pepper strips
1 teaspoon dried dill weed
   Dash ground red pepper
1 can (about 14 ounces) diced tomatoes, undrained
½ cup white wine
2 tablespoons lime juice
8 ounces swordfish steak, cut into 1-inch cubes
8 ounces bay or sea scallops, cut into quarters
1 bottle (8 ounces) clam juice
2 tablespoons cornstarch
2 cups frozen diced potatoes, thawed and drained
8 ounces frozen cooked medium shrimp, thawed and drained
½ cup whipping cream

1. Melt butter in Dutch oven over medium-high heat. Add onion, bell pepper, dill weed and red pepper; cook and stir 5 minutes or until vegetables are tender.

2. Reduce heat to medium. Add tomatoes with juice, wine and lime juice; bring to a boil. Add swordfish and scallops; cook and stir 2 minutes.

3. Combine clam juice and cornstarch in small bowl; stir until smooth.

4. Increase heat to high. Add potatoes, shrimp, whipping cream and clam juice mixture; bring to a boil. Season to taste with salt and black pepper.

Makes 6 servings

Prep and Cook Time: 20 minutes

Serving Suggestion: For a special touch, garnish stew with fresh lemon wedges.

Shrimp Veg•All® Pot Pie with Lemon Dill Crust

2 tablespoons butter
1 clove garlic, minced
⅓ cup white wine
2 cans (15 ounces each) VEG•ALL® Original Mixed Vegetables, drained and liquid reserved from 1 can
2 tablespoons cornstarch
2 tablespoons cold water
1 package (16 ounces) frozen cooked jumbo shrimp, peeled and deveined

Crust

1 egg, beaten
½ cup milk
1 cup biscuit mix
1 teaspoon grated lemon peel
1 teaspoon dill weed

Preheat oven to 400°F. In large skillet, melt butter. Add garlic and cook over medium-high heat. Stir in wine and reserved liquid from 1 can of Veg•All. In small bowl, blend cornstarch with water. Add to skillet and cook for 2 to 3 minutes, stirring constantly, until mixture bubbles and thickens. Remove from heat. Add Veg•All and shrimp to skillet; stir to combine. Pour into greased 2-quart casserole.

To make crust, in medium mixing bowl, combine egg and milk. Add biscuit mix, lemon peel, and dill; stir with fork until blended. Pour topping over vegetable mixture. Bake for 30 to 40 minutes or until heated through and crust is golden.   *Makes 6 servings*

Sweet and Sour Fish

⅓ cup GRANDMA'S® Molasses
¼ cup cider vinegar
¼ cup plus 2 tablespoons cornstarch, divided
2 tablespoons pineapple juice, reserved from chunks
2 tablespoons ketchup
2 tablespoons soy sauce
1 pound swordfish or red snapper, cut into 1-inch cubes
3 tablespoons vegetable oil, divided
1 green, red or yellow bell pepper, cut into strips
2 green onions, chopped
1 (8-ounce) can pineapple chunks in its own juice, drained, reserving
    2 tablespoons juice for sauce
Hot cooked rice or noodles
Cherry tomatoes, cut into halves

In medium bowl, combine molasses, vinegar, 2 tablespoons cornstarch,
2 tablespoons pineapple juice, ketchup and soy sauce; blend well. Set aside.
Coat swordfish with remaining ¼ cup cornstarch. In large skillet, heat
2 tablespoons oil. Stir-fry 5 minutes or until fish flakes easily with fork.
Remove from skillet. Heat remaining 1 tablespoon oil in skillet. Stir-fry bell
pepper and onions 2 minutes or until crisp-tender. Add molasses mixture;
cook until thickened. Add fish and pineapple; cook until heated through. Serve
over rice and garnish with tomatoes.   *Makes 4 servings*

Before measuring molasses, lightly coat a measuring
cup with nonstick cooking spray so the molasses will
slide out easily instead of clinging to the cup.

Sweet and Sour Fish

Tuna Noodle Casserole

  7 ounces uncooked elbow macaroni
  2 tablespoons butter
¾ cup chopped onion
½ cup thinly sliced celery
½ cup finely chopped red bell pepper
  2 tablespoons all-purpose flour
  1 teaspoon salt
⅛ teaspoon white pepper
1½ cups milk
  1 can (6 ounces) albacore tuna in water, drained
½ cup grated Parmesan cheese, divided
    Fresh dill sprigs (optional)

1. Preheat oven to 375°F. Spray 8-inch square baking dish with nonstick cooking spray.

2. Cook pasta according to package directions until al dente. Drain and set aside.

3. Meanwhile, melt butter in large deep skillet over medium heat. Add onion; cook and stir 3 minutes. Add celery and bell pepper; cook and stir 3 minutes. Sprinkle flour, salt and white pepper over vegetables; cook and stir 1 minute. Gradually stir in milk; cook and stir until thickened. Remove from heat.

4. Add pasta, tuna and ¼ cup cheese to skillet; stir until pasta is well coated. Pour tuna mixture into prepared dish; sprinkle evenly with remaining ¼ cup cheese.

5. Bake, uncovered, 20 to 25 minutes or until hot and bubbly. Garnish with dill, if desired.

Makes 4 servings

Tuna Noodle Casserole

Crab and Corn Enchilada Casserole

    Spicy Tomato Sauce (recipe follows), divided
10 to 12 ounces fresh crabmeat or flaked or chopped surimi crab
 1 package (10 ounces) frozen corn, thawed and drained
1½ cups (6 ounces) shredded Monterey Jack cheese, divided
 1 can (4 ounces) diced mild green chiles
12 (6-inch) corn tortillas
 1 lime, cut into 6 wedges
    Sour cream (optional)

Preheat oven to 350°F. Prepare Spicy Tomato Sauce.

Combine 2 cups Spicy Tomato Sauce, crabmeat, corn, 1 cup cheese and chiles in medium bowl. Cut each tortilla into 4 wedges. Place one third of tortilla wedges in shallow 3- to 4-quart casserole, overlapping to make solid layer. Spread half of crab mixture on top. Repeat with another layer of tortilla wedges, remaining crab mixture and remaining tortillas. Spread remaining 1 cup Spicy Tomato Sauce over top; cover.

Bake 30 to 40 minutes or until heated through. Sprinkle with remaining ½ cup cheese; bake uncovered 5 minutes or until cheese melts. Squeeze lime over individual servings. Serve with sour cream, if desired.   *Makes 6 servings*

Spicy Tomato Sauce

    2 cans (15 ounces each) stewed tomatoes, undrained *or* 6 medium tomatoes
    2 teaspoons olive oil
    1 medium onion, chopped
    1 tablespoon minced garlic
    2 tablespoons chili powder
    2 teaspoons *each* ground cumin and dried oregano
    1 teaspoon ground cinnamon
    ¼ teaspoon *each* red pepper flakes and ground cloves

Place tomatoes with juice in food processor or blender; process until finely chopped. Set aside.

Heat oil over medium-high heat in large saucepan or Dutch oven. Add onion and garlic. Cook and stir 5 minutes or until onion is tender. Add chili powder, cumin, oregano, cinnamon, pepper flakes and cloves. Cook and stir 1 minute. Add tomatoes; reduce heat to medium-low. Simmer, uncovered, 20 minutes or until sauce is reduced to 3 to 3¼ cups.   *Makes about 3 cups sauce*

Crab and Corn Enchilada Casserole

Cheesy Tuna Pie

2 cups cooked rice
2 cans (6 ounces each) tuna, drained and flaked
1 cup mayonnaise
1 cup (4 ounces) shredded Cheddar cheese
1 can (4 ounces) sliced black olives
½ cup thinly sliced celery
½ cup sour cream
2 tablespoons onion flakes
1 refrigerated pie crust dough

Preheat oven to 350°F. Spray 9-inch deep-dish pie pan with nonstick cooking spray. Combine all ingredients except pie dough in medium bowl; mix well. Spoon into prepared pie pan. Place pie dough over tuna mixture; press edge to pie pan to seal. Cut slits for steam to escape. Bake 20 minutes or until crust is browned and filling is bubbly. *Makes 6 servings*

Creamy Shrimp & Vegetable Casserole

1 can (10¾ ounces) condensed cream of celery soup, undiluted
1 pound fresh or thawed frozen shrimp, shelled and deveined
½ cup sliced fresh or thawed frozen asparagus (1-inch pieces)
½ cup sliced mushrooms
¼ cup sliced green onions
¼ cup diced red bell pepper
1 clove garlic, minced
¾ teaspoon dried thyme
¼ teaspoon black pepper
Hot cooked rice or orzo (optional)

1. Preheat oven to 375°F. Lightly grease 2-quart baking dish.

2. Combine soup, shrimp, asparagus, mushrooms, green onions, bell pepper, garlic, thyme and black pepper in large bowl; mix well. Place in prepared baking dish.

3. Cover and bake 30 minutes. Serve over rice, if desired. *Makes 4 servings*

Cheesy Tuna Pie

Tarragon Scallops & Zucchini

1¼ pounds sea scallops
6 tablespoons butter
2 small zucchini, thinly sliced
¼ teaspoon onion powder
2 cups uncooked instant white rice
3 large green onions, chopped
3 tablespoons chopped fresh tarragon *or* ¾ teaspoon dried tarragon
¼ teaspoon salt
2 tablespoons lemon juice
2 teaspoons cornstarch

1. Rinse scallops; pat dry with paper towels. Cut large scallops in half.

2. Melt butter in large nonstick skillet over medium heat. Stir in scallops, zucchini and onion powder; cook and stir 2 minutes. Cover; reduce heat. Cook 7 minutes.

3. Meanwhile, prepare rice according to package directions; set aside. Combine green onions, tarragon and salt in small bowl. Blend lemon juice and cornstarch in another small bowl until smooth; set aside.

4. Stir green onions and cornstarch mixture into skillet. Increase heat to medium; cook and stir 1 minute or until sauce thickens and scallops are opaque. Serve over rice.

Makes 4 servings

Prep and Cook Time: 20 minutes

When purchasing scallops, select those with a creamy white color, a shiny texture and a sweet smell. Scallops that appear to be stark white have been soaked in water and might not be the best buy for your money. Scallops should be used within one day of purchase to guarantee freshness. Cook scallops briefly to prevent overcooking, which tends to toughen them.

Tarragon Scallops & Zucchini

Curried Shrimp and Noodles

3 cups water

2 packages (about 1.6 ounces each) instant curry-flavored rice noodle soup mix

1 package (8 ounces) frozen cooked baby shrimp

1 cup frozen bell pepper strips, cut into 1-inch pieces *or* 1 cup frozen peas

¼ cup chopped green onions, green part only

¼ teaspoon salt

¼ teaspoon black pepper

1 to 2 tablespoons fresh lime juice

1. Place 3 cups water in large saucepan; bring to a boil over high heat. Add soup mix, shrimp, bell pepper, onions, salt and pepper.

2. Cook 3 to 5 minutes, stirring frequently, or until noodles are tender. Stir in lime juice. Serve immediately. *Makes 4 servings*

Fish Broccoli Casserole

1 package (10 ounces) frozen broccoli spears, thawed, drained

1 cup cooked flaked Florida whitefish

1 can (10¾ ounces) condensed cream of mushroom soup, undiluted

½ cup milk

¼ teaspoon salt

⅛ teaspoon freshly ground black pepper

½ cup crushed potato chips

Preheat oven to 425°F. Grease 1½-quart casserole. Layer broccoli in prepared casserole. Combine fish, soup, milk, salt and pepper in large bowl.

Spread fish mixture over broccoli. Sprinkle with potato chips. Bake 12 to 15 minutes or until golden brown. *Makes 4 servings*

*Favorite recipe from **Florida Department of Agriculture and Consumer Services, Bureau of Seafood and Aquaculture***

Curried Shrimp and Noodles

Elegant Fish and Seafood Stew

3 tablespoons vegetable oil
1 leek, sliced
1 medium green bell pepper, coarsely chopped
2 stalks celery, sliced
1 medium carrot, chopped
2 cloves garlic, minced
3 cups chicken broth or fish stock
1 can (about 14 ounces) tomatoes, cut-up and undrained
1 teaspoon Worcestershire sauce
½ teaspoon dried thyme
¼ teaspoon dried marjoram
1 bay leaf
¼ teaspoon salt (optional)
⅛ teaspoon black pepper
6 hard-shell clams, scrubbed and soaked
8 ounces fish fillets, such as red snapper, halibut or cod, skinned and cut
    into 1-inch pieces
8 ounces medium raw shrimp, peeled and deveined
6 to 8 ounces cooked crabmeat,* cleaned
    Toasted French bread slices (optional)

Cooked crab legs can be purchased for this recipe, if desired. One pound of legs will yield about 8 ounces of cooked crabmeat.

1. Heat oil in Dutch oven or large saucepan over medium heat. Cook and stir leek, bell pepper, celery, carrot and garlic 8 minutes or until vegetables are crisp-tender.

2. Add broth, tomatoes with juice, Worcestershire, thyme, marjoram, bay leaf, salt, if desired, and black pepper. Bring to a boil over high heat. Reduce heat to medium-low; simmer, uncovered, 15 minutes.

3. Add clams, fish, shrimp and crabmeat to vegetable mixture. Bring to a boil over high heat. Reduce heat to medium-low; cook about 8 minutes or until clams open and fish and shrimp are opaque. Discard bay leaf.

4. Serve stew in bowls (1 clam per serving) with toasted French bread slices, if desired.
Makes 6 servings

Elegant Fish and Seafood Stew

Salmon Linguini Supper

8 ounces linguini, cooked in unsalted water and drained
1 package (10 ounces) frozen peas
1 cup milk
1 can (10¾ ounces) condensed cream of celery soup, undiluted
¼ cup (1 ounce) grated Parmesan cheese
⅛ teaspoon dried tarragon, crumbled (optional)
1 can (15½ ounces) salmon, drained and flaked
1 egg, slightly beaten
¼ teaspoon salt
¼ teaspoon black pepper
1⅓ cups *French's*® French Fried Onions, divided

Preheat oven to 375°F. Return hot pasta to saucepan; stir in peas, milk, soup, cheese and tarragon; spoon into 12×8-inch baking dish. In medium bowl, using fork, combine salmon, egg, salt, pepper and ⅔ cup French Fried Onions. Shape salmon mixture into 4 oval patties. Place patties on pasta mixture. Bake, covered, at 375°F for 40 minutes or until patties are done. Top patties with remaining ⅔ *cup* onions; bake, uncovered, 3 minutes or until onions are golden brown.   *Makes 4 servings*

Microwave Directions: Prepare pasta mixture as above, except increase milk to 1¼ cups; spoon into 12×8-inch microwave-safe dish. Cook, covered, on HIGH 3 minutes; stir. Prepare salmon patties as above using 2 eggs. Place patties on pasta mixture. Cook, covered, 10 to 12 minutes or until patties are done. Rotate dish halfway through cooking time. Top patties with remaining onions; cook, uncovered, 1 minute. Let stand 5 minutes.

Curried Fish Casserole

Nonstick cooking spray
2 cups thinly sliced bok choy or napa cabbage
1 cup sliced red bell pepper, divided
½ cup uncooked quick-cooking brown rice
⅓ cup plus 3 tablespoons water, divided
4 (4 ounces each) Tilapia or white fish fillets, cleaned
½ teaspoon salt, divided
1 cup low-sodium chicken broth
1 teaspoon curry powder
¾ teaspoon sugar
1 tablespoon cornstarch
¼ cup finely chopped green onions (optional)

1. Preheat oven to 350°F. Spray 13×9-inch baking pan with cooking spray. Add bok choy, ½ cup bell pepper, rice and ⅓ cup water; toss gently to blend.

2. Arrange fillets over vegetables; sprinkle with ¼ teaspoon salt. Cover with foil; bake 30 minutes or until fish flakes easily with fork.

3. Meanwhile, combine broth, remaining bell pepper, curry powder, sugar and remaining ¼ teaspoon salt in small saucepan. Bring to a boil over medium-high heat; cook and stir 1 minute.

4. Combine cornstarch and remaining 3 tablespoons water in small bowl; stir until completely dissolved. Add to curry mixture; cook and stir 1 minute, scraping bottom and side of pan to prevent sticking.

5. Portion fish and rice mixture on 4 dinner plates; spoon equal amounts of sauce over each. Top with green onions, if desired. *Makes 4 servings*

Shrimp Creole

2 tablespoons olive oil
1½ cups chopped green bell pepper
1 medium onion, chopped
⅔ cup chopped celery
2 cloves garlic, finely chopped
1 cup uncooked rice
1 can (14½ ounces) diced tomatoes, drained and juice reserved
2 teaspoons hot pepper sauce, or to taste
1 teaspoon dried oregano
¾ teaspoon salt
½ teaspoon dried thyme
   Black pepper to taste
1 pound medium raw shrimp, peeled and deveined
1 tablespoon chopped fresh parsley (optional)

1. Preheat oven to 325°F. Heat olive oil in large skillet over medium-high heat. Add bell pepper, onion, celery and garlic; cook and stir 5 minutes or until vegetables are tender.

2. Add rice; cook and stir 5 minutes over medium heat. Add tomatoes, hot sauce, oregano, salt, thyme and black pepper to skillet; stir until blended. Pour reserved tomato juice into measuring cup. Add enough water to measure 1¾ cups liquid; add to skillet. Cook and stir 2 minutes.

3. Transfer mixture to 2½-quart casserole. Stir in shrimp. Bake, covered, 55 minutes or until rice is tender and liquid is absorbed. Sprinkle with fresh parsley, if desired. *Makes 4 to 6 servings*

Shrimp Creole

Crab-Artichoke Casserole

8 ounces uncooked small shell pasta
2 tablespoons butter
6 green onions, chopped
2 tablespoons all-purpose flour
1 cup half-and-half
1 teaspoon dry mustard
½ teaspoon ground red pepper
   Salt and black pepper
½ cup (2 ounces) shredded Swiss cheese, divided
1 package (about 8 ounces) imitation crabmeat
1 can (about 14 ounces) artichoke hearts, drained and cut into bite-size
   pieces

1. Preheat oven to 350°F. Grease 2-quart casserole. Cook pasta according to package directions; drain and set aside.

2. Melt butter in large saucepan over medium heat. Add green onions; cook and stir about 2 minutes. Add flour; cook and stir 2 minutes more. Gradually add half-and-half, whisking constantly until mixture begins to thicken. Whisk in mustard and red pepper; season to taste with salt and black pepper. Remove from heat; stir in ¼ cup cheese until melted.

3. Combine crabmeat, artichokes and pasta in prepared casserole. Add sauce mixture; stir until blended. Top with remaining ¼ cup cheese. Bake about 40 minutes or until hot, bubbly and lightly browned.   *Makes 6 servings*

This delicious casserole can also be baked in individual ovenproof dishes. Reduce the cooking time to about 20 minutes.

Albacore Stir-Fry

    3 tablespoons vegetable oil
    ½ cup sliced onion
    1 clove garlic, minced or pressed
    1 bag (16 ounces) frozen Oriental vegetables, thawed and drained*
    1 (7-ounce) STARKIST Flavor Fresh Pouch® Tuna (Albacore)
    3 tablespoons soy sauce
    1 tablespoon lemon juice
    1 tablespoon water
    1 teaspoon sugar
    2 cups hot cooked rice

You can use 4 cups fresh vegetables, such as carrots, pea pods, broccoli, bell peppers, mushrooms, celery and bean sprouts instead of the frozen vegetables.

In wok or large skillet, heat oil over medium-high heat; sauté onion and garlic until onion is soft. Add vegetables; cook about 3 to 4 minutes or until vegetables are crisp-tender. Add tuna, soy sauce, lemon juice, water and sugar. Cook 1 more minute; serve over rice.   *Makes 4 servings*

Lemon Shrimp

    1 package (12 ounces) uncooked egg noodles
    ½ cup (1 stick) butter, softened
    2 pounds cooked shrimp
    3 tomatoes, chopped
    1 cup chicken broth
    1 cup shredded carrots
    1 can (4 ounces) sliced mushrooms, drained
    2 tablespoons fresh lemon juice
    2 cloves garlic, chopped
    ½ teaspoon celery seed
    ¼ teaspoon black pepper

1. Preheat oven to 350°F.

2. Cook noodles according to package directions. Drain; toss with butter in large bowl until butter is melted and noodles are evenly coated. Stir in remaining ingredients. Transfer to 3-quart casserole.

3. Bake 15 to 20 minutes or until heated through.   *Makes 8 servings*

Albacore Stir-Fry

Stir-Fried Catfish with Cucumber Rice

1 seedless cucumber
1¼ cups water
½ cup uncooked rice
4 green onions, thinly sliced
½ teaspoon white pepper
2 teaspoons canola oil
1 pound catfish fillets, cut into 1-inch chunks
1 teaspoon minced fresh ginger
1 clove garlic, minced
¼ teaspoon dark sesame oil
2 packages (6 ounces each) snow peas
1 red bell pepper, diced
¼ cup white wine or water
1 tablespoon cornstarch

1. Grate cucumber on medium side of grater into colander set over bowl; drain.

2. Combine water, rice, cucumber, green onions and white pepper in medium saucepan. Bring to a boil over medium heat. Cover; reduce heat to low. Cook about 20 minutes or until rice is tender and liquid is absorbed.

3. Heat oil in 12-inch nonstick skillet over high heat. Add catfish, ginger, garlic and sesame oil. Stir-fry 4 to 5 minutes or until catfish is just cooked. Add snow peas and bell pepper. Cover and cook 4 minutes.

4. Meanwhile, combine wine and cornstarch in small bowl; stir. Pour mixture over catfish mixture; cook and stir about 2 minutes or until sauce thickens. Serve over rice.   *Makes 4 servings*

Serving Suggestion: Serve with Egg Drop Soup made by stirring beaten egg into simmering chicken broth seasoned with your favorite fresh chopped herbs, such as cilantro. Complete the meal with chilled fresh seasonal fruit cups or a scoop of lemon sorbet.

Stir-Fried Catfish with Cucumber Rice

Tuna Tomato Casserole

2 cans (6 ounces each) tuna, drained
1 cup mayonnaise
1 small onion, finely chopped
¼ teaspoon salt
¼ teaspoon black pepper
1 package (12 ounces) uncooked wide egg noodles
8 to 10 plum tomatoes, sliced ¼ inch thick
1 cup (4 ounces) shredded Cheddar or mozzarella cheese

Preheat oven to 375°F. Combine tuna, mayonnaise, onion, salt and pepper in medium bowl; mix well. Cook noodles according to package directions, cooking just until tender. Drain noodles and return to saucepan. Add tuna mixture to noodles; stir until well blended. Layer half of noodle mixture, half of tomatoes and half of cheese in 13×9-inch baking dish. Press down slightly. Repeat layers with remaining ingredients. Bake 20 minutes or until cheese is melted and casserole is heated through. *Makes 6 servings*

Biscuit-Topped Tuna Bake

2 tablespoons vegetable oil
½ cup chopped onion
½ cup chopped celery
1 can (10¾ ounces) condensed cream of potato soup, undiluted
1 package (10 ounces) frozen peas and carrots, thawed
1 (7-ounce) STARKIST Flavor Fresh Pouch® Tuna (Albacore or Chunk Light)
¾ cup milk
¼ teaspoon garlic powder
¼ teaspoon ground black pepper
1 can (7½ ounces) refrigerator flaky biscuits

In large skillet, heat oil over medium-high heat; sauté onion and celery until onion is soft. Add remaining ingredients except biscuits; heat thoroughly. Transfer mixture to 1½-quart casserole. Arrange biscuits around top edge of dish; bake in 400°F oven 10 to 15 minutes or until biscuits are golden brown. *Makes 4 to 6 servings*

Prep and Cook Time: 25 minutes

Tuna Tomato Casserole

Zesty Shrimp Primavera

8 ounces uncooked angel hair pasta
1 tablespoon olive oil
2 cups thinly sliced carrot sticks
2 cups thin strips red bell pepper
2 small zucchini, thinly sliced
3 cloves garlic, minced and divided
½ teaspoon crushed red pepper flakes
2 tablespoons butter
1½ pounds medium raw shrimp, peeled and deveined
¼ cup grated Parmesan cheese
1 tablespoon fresh chopped basil or parsley

1. Cook pasta according to package directions. Drain; place in large shallow pasta bowl and keep warm.

2. Heat oil in large nonstick skillet over medium high heat. Add carrots, bell peppers, zucchini, 1 teaspoon garlic and red pepper flakes. Cook and stir 5 minutes or until carrots are crisp-tender. Add to pasta.

3. Melt butter in same skillet over medium heat. Add shrimp and remaining garlic. Cook and stir 2 to 3 minutes until shrimp turn pink. Return pasta and vegetables to skillet. Add Parmesan cheese. Stir gently until well blended. Return to pasta bowl; sprinkle with basil.   *Makes 6 servings*

To devein shrimp, cut a shallow slit along the back of the shrimp with a paring knife. Lift out the vein. (You may find this easier to do under cold running water.) The veins of large and jumbo shrimp are gritty; they must always be removed. The veins of medium and small shrimp are not gritty and need not be removed unless you wish a more elegant presentation.

Zesty Shrimp Primavera

Broccoli-Stuffed Shells

1 tablespoon butter or margarine
¼ cup chopped onion
1 cup ricotta cheese
1 egg
2 cups chopped cooked broccoli *or* 1 package (10 ounces) frozen chopped broccoli, thawed and well drained
1 cup (4 ounces) shredded Monterey Jack cheese
20 jumbo pasta shells
1 can (28 ounces) crushed tomatoes in purée
1 packet (1 ounce) HIDDEN VALLEY® The Original Ranch® Salad Dressing & Seasoning Mix
¼ cup grated Parmesan cheese

Preheat oven to 350°F. In small skillet, melt butter over medium heat. Add onion; cook until onion is tender but not browned. Remove from heat; cool. In large bowl, stir ricotta cheese and egg until well blended. Add broccoli and Monterey Jack cheese; mix well. In large pot of boiling water, cook pasta shells 8 to 10 minutes or just until tender; drain. Rinse under cold running water; drain again. Stuff each shell with about 2 tablespoons broccoli-cheese mixture.

In medium bowl, combine tomatoes, sautéed onion and salad dressing & seasoning mix; mix well. Pour one third of the tomato mixture into 13×9-inch baking dish. Arrange filled shells in dish. Spoon remaining tomato mixture over top. Sprinkle with Parmesan cheese. Bake, covered, until hot and bubbly, about 30 minutes.

Makes 4 servings

Broccoli-Stuffed Shells

Fresh Vegetable Casserole

8 small new potatoes
8 baby carrots
1 small head cauliflower, broken into florets
4 stalks asparagus, cut into 1-inch pieces
3 tablespoons butter
3 tablespoons all-purpose flour
2 cups milk
  Salt
  Black pepper
¾ cup (3 ounces) shredded Cheddar cheese
  Chopped fresh cilantro

1. Steam vegetables until crisp-tender. Arrange vegetables in buttered 2-quart casserole. Preheat oven to 350°F.

2. To make sauce, melt butter in medium saucepan over medium heat. Stir in flour until smooth. Gradually stir in milk. Cook until thickened, stirring constantly. Season to taste with salt and pepper. Add cheese, stirring until cheese is melted. Pour sauce over vegetables and sprinkle with cilantro. Bake 15 minutes or until heated through. *Makes 4 to 6 servings*

New potatoes are freshly dug young potatoes. They may be any variety, but most often are round reds. New potatoes can be as small as marbles or almost as large as full-size potatoes, but they should have a very thin wispy skin. The sugar in these young potatoes has not completely converted to starch so they have a crisp, waxy texture.

Fresh Vegetable Casserole

Italian Vegetable Stew

1 teaspoon olive oil
2 medium zucchini, halved lengthwise and thinly sliced
1 medium eggplant, chopped
1 large onion, thinly sliced
⅛ teaspoon ground black pepper
1 jar (1 pound 10 ounces) RAGÚ® Light Pasta Sauce
3 tablespoons grated Parmesan cheese
1 box (10 ounces) couscous

1. In 12-inch nonstick skillet, heat olive oil over medium heat and cook zucchini, eggplant, onion and pepper, stirring occasionally, 15 minutes or until vegetables are golden.

2. Stir in Ragú Pasta Sauce and cheese. Bring to a boil over high heat. Reduce heat to low and simmer covered 10 minutes.

3. Meanwhile, prepare couscous according to package directions. Serve vegetable mixture over hot couscous.   *Makes 4 servings*

Prep Time: 10 minutes
Cook Time: 25 minutes

Italian Vegetable Stew

Black Bean Vegetarian Chili

1 tablespoon olive oil
2 onions, finely chopped and divided
1 green bell pepper, diced
1 teaspoon ground cumin
1 teaspoon minced garlic
1 to 2 canned chipotle peppers, stemmed and diced, seeds included*
4 cans (15 ounces each) black beans, rinsed and drained
1 can (15 ounces) corn, drained
1 can (15 ounces) diced tomatoes, undrained
1 can (6 ounces) tomato paste plus 3 cans water
½ teaspoon salt
½ teaspoon black pepper
  Sour cream
  Whole wheat flour tortillas (optional)

Chipotle peppers come in 7-ounce cans packed in adobo sauce. Use 1 pepper for mildly spicy chili, 2 for very spicy. Unused peppers and sauce can be frozen in small plastic bags for later use.

1. Heat olive oil in Dutch oven until hot. Reserve ½ cup chopped onions. Add remaining onions and bell pepper to Dutch oven; cook and stir 5 minutes or until soft. Add cumin; cook and stir about 10 seconds. Add garlic; cook and stir 1 minute.

2. Stir in chipotle peppers, black beans, corn, tomatoes with juice, tomato paste, water, salt and black pepper. Bring to a boil. Reduce heat and simmer 30 minutes.

3. Serve with sour cream, reserved onions and whole wheat flour tortillas, if desired.   *Makes 8 servings*

Black Bean Vegetarian Chili

Eggplant Pasta Bake

4 ounces dry bow-tie pasta
1 pound eggplant, diced
1 clove garlic, minced
¼ cup olive oil
1½ cups shredded Monterey Jack cheese, divided
1 cup sliced green onions
½ cup grated Parmesan cheese
1 can (14½ ounces) DEL MONTE® Diced Tomatoes with Basil, Garlic & Oregano, undrained

1. Preheat oven to 350°F. Cook pasta according to package directions; drain.

2. Cook eggplant and garlic in oil in large skillet over medium-high heat until tender.

3. Toss eggplant with cooked pasta, 1 cup Jack cheese, green onions and Parmesan cheese.

4. Place in greased 9-inch square baking dish. Top with undrained tomatoes and remaining ½ cup Jack cheese. Bake 15 minutes or until heated through.

Makes 6 servings

Prep and Cook Time: 30 minutes

When purchasing eggplant, choose a firm, smooth-skinned eggplant
that feels heavy for its size. The skin should be tight, glossy and a
deep purple color. The stem should be bright green and look fresh.
Dull skin and rust-colored blemishes or soft spots are a sign of old age.
Usually, the smaller the eggplant, the sweeter and more tender it is.
Refrigerate unwashed eggplant in a plastic bag for up to 5 days.

Broccoli-Tofu Stir-Fry

2 cups uncooked rice
1 can (14½ ounces) vegetable broth, divided
3 tablespoons cornstarch
1 tablespoon reduced-sodium soy sauce
½ teaspoon sugar
¼ teaspoon dark sesame oil
1 package (16 ounces) extra-firm tofu, well drained*
1 teaspoon peanut oil
1 tablespoon minced fresh ginger
3 cloves garlic, minced
3 cups broccoli florets
2 cups sliced mushrooms
½ cup chopped green onions
1 large red bell pepper, seeded and cut into strips
  Prepared Szechwan sauce (optional)

Tofu must be drained before being stir-fried. Remove any remaining water by placing the block of tofu on several layers of paper towels and covering it with additional paper towels weighted down with a heavy plate. Let it stand for 15 to 20 minutes before cutting into cubes.

1. Cook rice according to package directions. Combine ¼ cup vegetable broth, cornstarch, soy sauce, sugar and sesame oil in small bowl; set aside. Cut tofu into 1-inch cubes; set aside.

2. Heat peanut oil in large nonstick wok or skillet over medium heat until hot. Add ginger and garlic. Cook and stir 5 minutes. Add remaining vegetable broth, broccoli, mushrooms, green onions and bell pepper. Cook and stir over medium-high heat 5 minutes or until vegetables are crisp-tender. Add tofu; cook 2 minutes, stirring occasionally. Stir cornstarch mixture; add to vegetable mixture. Cook and stir until sauce thickens. Serve over rice with Szechwan sauce and garnish, if desired. *Makes 6 servings*

Hearty Manicotti

8 to 10 dry manicotti shells
1 package (10 ounces) frozen chopped spinach, thawed, squeezed dry
1 carton (15 ounces) ricotta cheese
1 egg, lightly beaten
½ cup (2 ounces) grated Parmesan cheese
⅛ teaspoon ground black pepper
2 cans (6 ounces each) CONTADINA® Italian Paste with Italian
    Seasonings
1⅓ cups water
½ cup (2 ounces) shredded mozzarella cheese

1. Cook pasta according to package directions; drain.

2. Meanwhile, combine spinach, ricotta cheese, egg, Parmesan cheese and pepper in medium bowl; mix well.

3. Spoon into manicotti shells. Place in ungreased 12×7½-inch baking dish.

4. Combine tomato paste and water in small bowl; pour over manicotti. Sprinkle with mozzarella cheese. Bake in preheated 350°F oven for 30 to 40 minutes or until heated through.   *Makes 4 to 5 servings*

Prep Time: 15 minutes
Cook Time: 40 minutes

Hearty Manicotti

Layered Mexican Tortilla Cheese Casserole

1 can (14½ ounces) salsa-style or Mexican-style stewed tomatoes, undrained
½ cup chopped fresh cilantro, divided
2 tablespoons fresh lime juice
    Nonstick vegetable cooking spray
6 (6-inch) corn tortillas, torn into 1½-inch pieces
1 can (15 ounces) black beans, rinsed and drained
1 can (8 ounces) whole kernel corn, drained *or* 1 cup frozen whole kernel corn, thawed
2 cups (8 ounces) SARGENTO® Mexican Blend Shredded Cheese

1. In small bowl, combine tomatoes, ¼ cup cilantro and lime juice; set aside.

2. Coat 8-inch square baking dish with cooking spray. Arrange one fourth of tortillas in bottom of dish; spoon one fourth of tomato mixture over tortillas. Top with one fourth of beans, one fourth of corn and one fourth of cheese. Repeat layering 3 more times with remaining tortillas, tomato mixture, beans, corn and cheese.

3. Bake uncovered at 375°F 25 minutes or until cheese is melted and sauce is bubbly. Sprinkle with remaining ¼ cup cilantro. Let stand 10 minutes before serving.
Makes 4 servings

To get the most juice from a fresh lime, start with one that is at room temperature, then roll it around on the counter under the palm of your hand. This releases juice from the small juice-filled sacs. Cut it in half and use a reamer or juicer, either hand or electric, to extract the juice.

Layered Mexican Tortilla Cheese Casserole

Baked Risotto with Asparagus, Spinach & Parmesan

1 tablespoon olive oil
1 cup finely chopped onion
1 cup arborio rice
8 cups (8 to 10 ounces) spinach leaves, torn into pieces
2 cups vegetable broth
¼ teaspoon salt
¼ teaspoon ground nutmeg
½ cup grated Parmesan cheese, divided
1½ cups diagonally sliced asparagus

1. Preheat oven to 400°F. Spray 13×9-inch baking dish with nonstick cooking spray.

2. Heat olive oil in large skillet over medium-high heat. Add onion; cook and stir 4 minutes or until tender. Add rice; stir to coat with oil.

3. Stir in spinach, a handful at a time, adding more as it wilts. Add broth, salt and nutmeg. Reduce heat and simmer 7 minutes. Stir in ¼ cup cheese.

4. Transfer to prepared baking dish. Cover tightly and bake 15 minutes.

5. Remove from oven and stir in asparagus; sprinkle with remaining ¼ cup cheese. Cover and bake 15 minutes more or until liquid is absorbed.

Makes 6 servings

*Baked Risotto with Asparagus,
Spinach & Parmesan*

Orange-Ginger Tofu & Noodles

⅔ cup orange juice

3 tablespoons reduced-sodium soy sauce

½ to 1 teaspoon minced fresh ginger

1 clove garlic, minced

¼ teaspoon red pepper flakes

5 ounces extra-firm tofu, well drained and cut into ½-inch cubes*

1½ teaspoons cornstarch

1 teaspoon canola or peanut oil

2 cups fresh cut-up vegetables, such as broccoli, carrots, onion and snow peas

1½ cups hot cooked vermicelli

Tofu must be drained before being stir-fried. Remove any remaining water by placing the block of tofu on several layers of paper towels and covering it with additional paper towels weighted down with a heavy plate. Let it stand for 15 to 20 minutes before cutting into cubes.

1. Combine orange juice, soy sauce, ginger, garlic and red pepper flakes in resealable food storage bag; add tofu. Marinate 20 to 30 minutes. Drain tofu, reserving marinade. Stir marinade into cornstarch until smooth.

2. Heat oil in large nonstick skillet or wok over medium-high heat. Add vegetables; stir-fry 2 to 3 minutes or until vegetables are crisp-tender. Add tofu; stir-fry 1 minute. Stir reserved marinade mixture; add to skillet. Bring to a boil; boil 1 minute. Serve over vermicelli.   *Makes 2 servings*

Tofu, also known as soybean curd, is made by coagulating soy milk, draining it and pressing the curds in a method similar to cheesemaking. Tofu is white or cream-colored with a creamy smooth texture and has a bland, slightly nutty taste. It is available in three forms: soft, firm and extra firm. Soft tofu can be whipped or blended for use in dips, fillings and scrambled eggs. Firm and extra-firm tofu can be cubed and used in stir-fries. Fresh tofu is packed in water and is available in the refrigerated section of many large supermarkets. It should be stored refrigerated and covered with water. The water should be changed daily. Fresh tofu will keep up to a week.

Orange-Ginger Tofu & Noodles

Tuscan Vegetable Stew

2 tablespoons olive oil

2 teaspoons minced garlic

2 packages (4 ounces each) sliced mixed exotic mushrooms *or* 1 package (8 ounces) sliced button mushrooms

¼ cup sliced shallots or chopped sweet onion

1 jar (7 ounces) roasted red peppers

1 can (14½ ounces) Italian-style stewed tomatoes, undrained

1 can (19 ounces) cannellini beans, rinsed and drained

1 bunch fresh basil*

1 tablespoon balsamic vinegar

Salt and black pepper

Grated Romano, Parmesan or Asiago cheese

*If fresh basil is not available, add 2 teaspoons dried basil to stew with tomatoes.

1. Heat oil and garlic in large deep skillet over medium heat. Add mushrooms and shallots; cook and stir 5 minutes.

2. Meanwhile, drain and rinse peppers; cut into 1-inch pieces. Snip tomatoes in can into small pieces with scissors.

3. Add tomatoes, peppers and beans to skillet; bring to a boil. Reduce heat to medium-low. Cover and simmer 10 minutes, stirring once.

4. Meanwhile, cut basil leaves into thin strips to measure ¼ cup. Stir basil and vinegar into stew; add salt and black pepper to taste. Sprinkle each serving with cheese. *Makes 4 servings*

Prep and Cook Time: 18 minutes

Tuscan Vegetable Stew

Moroccan Supper

1 (7.2-ounce) package RICE-A-RONI® Rice Pilaf
½ cup chopped onion
2 cloves garlic, minced
2 tablespoons margarine or olive oil
1 teaspoon ground cumin
¼ teaspoon ground cinnamon
1 (15-ounce) can garbanzo beans or chick peas, rinsed and drained
1½ cups broccoli flowerets
¼ cup dried apricots, slivered or raisins
⅓ cup slivered or sliced almonds, toasted
¼ cup chopped cilantro (optional)

1. In large skillet over medium heat, sauté rice-pasta mix, onion and garlic with margarine until pasta is light golden brown.

2. Slowly stir in 2 cups water, cumin, cinnamon and Special Seasonings; bring to a boil. Cover; reduce heat to low. Simmer 10 minutes.

3. Stir in beans, broccoli and apricots. Cover; simmer 10 to 12 minutes or until rice is tender. Serve topped with almonds and cilantro, if desired.

Makes 4 servings

Prep Time: 10 minutes
Cook Time: 30 minutes

Tip: For a Southwestern flair, use black beans, 1½ cups corn and ¼ teaspoon chili powder instead of garbanzo beans, apricots and cinnamon.

Three-Bean Caribbean Chili

1 tablespoon olive oil
1 large onion, chopped
2 cloves garlic, minced
1 jalapeño pepper,* seeded and minced
2 large red or green bell peppers, diced
1 tablespoon plus 2 teaspoons *each* sweet paprika and chili powder
2 teaspoons *each* sugar and ground cumin
½ teaspoon salt
¼ teaspoon ground cloves
3 cups water
1 can (6 ounces) tomato paste
1 can (15 ounces) cannellini beans, drained
1 can (15 ounces) red kidney beans, drained
1 can (15 ounces) black beans, drained
1 tablespoon balsamic vinegar
  Mango Salsa (recipe follows)
  Hot cooked brown rice

Jalapeño peppers can sting and irritate the skin, so wear rubber gloves when handling peppers and do not touch your eyes.

Heat oil in large saucepan over medium heat until hot. Add onion and garlic; cook and stir 4 minutes. Add jalapeño and bell peppers; cook and stir 5 minutes or until tender. Add paprika, chili powder, sugar, cumin, salt and cloves; cook and stir 1 minute. Stir in water and tomato paste until blended. Bring to a boil over high heat. Reduce heat to low. Cover; simmer 15 minutes. Stir in beans and vinegar; partially cover and simmer 15 minutes or until hot. Meanwhile, prepare Mango Salsa. Serve chili over brown rice. Top with Mango Salsa. Garnish as desired. *Makes 6 (1-cup) servings*

Mango Salsa

1 large mango, peeled and cut into ¾-inch cubes
1 small firm ripe banana, peeled and cubed
3 tablespoons minced fresh cilantro
1 tablespoon thawed frozen orange juice concentrate
1 teaspoon balsamic vinegar

Combine mango, banana and cilantro in medium bowl. Stir together juice concentrate and vinegar. Pour over fruit; toss. *Makes 1¼ cups salsa*

Indian Vegetable Curry

2 to 3 teaspoons curry powder
1 can (16 ounces) sliced potatoes, drained
1 bag (16 ounces) BIRDS EYE® frozen Broccoli, Cauliflower and Carrots
1 can (15 ounces) chick-peas, drained
1 can (14½ ounces) stewed tomatoes
1 can (13¾ ounces) vegetable or chicken broth
2 tablespoons cornstarch

• Stir curry powder in large skillet over high heat until fragrant, about 30 seconds.

• Stir in potatoes, vegetables, chick-peas and tomatoes; bring to a boil. Reduce heat to medium-high; cover and cook 8 minutes.

• Blend broth with cornstarch; stir into vegetables. Cook until thickened.

Makes about 6 servings

Prep Time: 5 minutes
Cook Time: 15 minutes

Serving Suggestion: Add cooked chicken for a heartier main dish. Serve with white or brown rice.

Curry can refer to both a wide range of hot, spicy sauce-based dishes of the East Indian cuisine and the integral spice blend used to make them. The characteristically bright yellow spice blend known as curry powder is based on garam masala, the Indian spice mixture prepared by pounding or grinding dried spices together. The mixture varies greatly as Indian cooks each make their own unique blends. Common ingredients for curry powder are cinnamon, cardamom, cloves, cumin, coriander, turmeric and ground red or black pepper. Curry powder is seldom prepared from scratch in the American kitchen and is readily available in grocery stores.

Indian Vegetable Curry

Ratatouille Pot Pie

¼ cup olive oil

1 medium eggplant (about 1 pound), peeled and cut into ½-inch pieces

1 large onion, chopped

1 green or yellow bell pepper, chopped

1½ teaspoons minced garlic

1 can (about 14 ounces) pasta-ready diced tomatoes with garlic and herbs or Italian stewed tomatoes, undrained

1 teaspoon dried basil

½ teaspoon red pepper flakes

¼ teaspoon salt

1 tablespoon balsamic vinegar

2 cups (8 ounces) shredded mozzarella cheese, divided

1 package (10 ounces) refrigerated pizza dough

1. Preheat oven to 425°F. Heat oil in large skillet over medium heat until hot. Add eggplant, onion, bell pepper and garlic. Cook 10 minutes or until eggplant begins to brown, stirring occasionally. Stir in tomatoes with juice, basil, red pepper flakes and salt. Cook, uncovered, over medium-low heat 5 minutes.

2. Remove from heat; stir in vinegar. Let stand 10 minutes; stir in 1 cup cheese. Transfer mixture to ungreased 11×7-inch casserole dish. Sprinkle with remaining cheese.

3. Unroll pizza dough; arrange over top of casserole. Make decorative cut-outs using small cookie cutter, if desired. Spray dough with nonstick cooking spray. Bake 15 minutes or until crust is golden brown and vegetable mixture is bubbly. Let stand 5 minutes before serving. *Makes 6 servings*

Ratatouille Pot Pie

Lasagna Florentine

2 tablespoons olive oil
3 medium carrots, finely chopped
1 package (8 to 10 ounces) sliced mushrooms
1 medium onion, finely chopped
2 cloves garlic, finely chopped
1 jar (1 pound 10 ounces) RAGÚ® Robusto®! Pasta Sauce
1 container (15 ounces) ricotta cheese
2 cups (8 ounces) shredded mozzarella cheese, divided
1 box (10 ounces) frozen chopped spinach, thawed and squeezed dry
2 eggs
¼ cup grated Parmesan cheese
1 teaspoon salt
1 teaspoon dried Italian seasoning
16 lasagna noodles, cooked and drained

1. Preheat oven to 375°F. In 12-inch skillet, heat olive oil over medium heat. Cook carrots, mushrooms, onion and garlic until carrots are almost tender, about 5 minutes. Stir in Pasta Sauce; heat through.

2. Meanwhile, in medium bowl, combine ricotta cheese, 1½ cups mozzarella cheese, spinach, eggs, Parmesan cheese, salt and Italian seasoning; set aside.

3. In 13×9-inch baking dish, evenly spread ½ cup sauce mixture. Arrange 4 lasagna noodles, lengthwise over sauce, overlapping edges slightly. Spread one third of ricotta mixture over noodles; repeat layers, ending with noodles. Top with remaining sauce and ½ cup mozzarella cheese. Cover with foil and bake 40 minutes. Remove foil and continue baking 10 minutes or until bubbling.

Makes 8 servings

Lasagna Florentine

Chunky Vegetable Chili

2 tablespoons vegetable oil
1 medium onion, chopped
2 stalks celery, diced
1 carrot, diced
3 cloves garlic, minced
2 cans (about 15 ounces each) Great Northern beans, rinsed and drained
1½ cups water
1 cup frozen corn
1 can (6 ounces) tomato paste
1 can (4 ounces) diced mild green chiles, undrained
1 tablespoon chili powder
2 teaspoons dried oregano
1 teaspoon salt

1. Heat oil in large skillet over medium-high heat until hot. Add onion, celery, carrot and garlic; cook 5 minutes or until vegetables are tender, stirring occasionally.

2. Stir beans, water, corn, tomato paste, chiles, chili powder, oregano and salt into skillet. Reduce heat to medium-low. Simmer 20 minutes, stirring occasionally. Garnish as desired.   *Makes 8 servings*

Chunky Vegetable Chili

Szechuan Vegetable Stir-Fry

8 ounces firm tofu, drained and cut into cubes*
1 cup vegetable broth, divided
½ cup orange juice
⅓ cup soy sauce
1 to 2 teaspoons hot chili oil
½ teaspoon whole fennel seeds
½ teaspoon black pepper
2 tablespoons cornstarch
3 tablespoons vegetable oil
1 cup sliced green onions and tops
3 medium carrots, peeled and diagonally sliced
3 cloves garlic, minced
2 teaspoons minced fresh ginger
¼ pound button mushrooms, sliced
1 medium red bell pepper, cut into 1-inch squares
¼ pound fresh snow peas, cut diagonally in half
8 ounces broccoli florets, steamed
½ cup peanuts
4 to 6 cups hot cooked rice

Tofu must be drained before being stir-fried. Remove any remaining water by placing the block of tofu on several layers of paper towels and covering it with additional paper towels weighted down with a heavy plate. Let it stand for 15 to 20 minutes before cutting into cubes.

1. Place tofu in 8-inch round or square baking dish. Combine ½ cup broth, orange juice, soy sauce, chili oil, fennel seeds and black pepper in small bowl; pour over tofu. Let stand 15 to 60 minutes. Drain, reserving marinade.

2. Combine cornstarch and remaining ½ cup broth in medium bowl. Add reserved marinade; set aside.

3. Heat vegetable oil in wok or large skillet over high heat until hot. Add onions, carrots, garlic and ginger; stir-fry 3 minutes. Add tofu, mushrooms, bell pepper and snow peas; stir-fry 2 to 3 minutes or until vegetables are crisp-tender. Add broccoli; stir-fry 1 minute or until heated through.

4. Stir cornstarch mixture. Add to wok; cook 1 to 2 minutes or until bubbly. Stir in peanuts. Serve over rice. *Makes 4 to 6 servings*

Szechuan Vegetable Stir-Fry

Lasagna Primavera

1 (8-ounce) package lasagna noodles
3 carrots, cut into ¼-inch slices
1 cup broccoli flowerets
1 cup zucchini, cut into ¼-inch slices
1 crookneck squash, cut into ¼-inch slices
2 (10-ounce) packages frozen chopped spinach, thawed
1 (8-ounce) container ricotta cheese
1 (26-ounce) jar NEWMAN'S OWN® Marinara Sauce with Mushrooms
3 cups (12 ounces) shredded mozzarella cheese
½ cup (2 ounces) grated Parmesan cheese

Bring 3 quarts water to a boil in a 6-quart saucepan over high heat. Add lasagna noodles and cook 5 minutes. Add carrots; cook 2 more minutes. Add broccoli, zucchini and crookneck squash; cook 2 minutes or until pasta is tender. Drain well.

Squeeze liquid out of spinach. Combine spinach and ricotta cheese. In a 3-quart rectangular baking pan, spread one third of the Newman's Own® Marinara Sauce with Mushrooms. Line pan with lasagna noodles. Layer half each of the vegetables, spinach mixture and mozzarella cheese over the noodles; top with half of the remaining Newman's Own® Marinara Sauce with Mushrooms. Repeat layers. Sprinkle with Parmesan cheese.

Place baking pan on 10×15-inch baking sheet which has been lined with foil. Bake uncovered in a 400°F oven about 30 minutes or until hot in the center. Let stand 10 minutes before serving. (Casserole may be prepared up to 2 days before baking. Refrigerate, covered, until 1 hour before baking. If cold, bake for 1 hour at 350°F.)   *Makes 8 servings*

Primavera is an Italian word meaning "springtime."
It is used as a term in the title of recipes that contain
fresh spring vegetables, either raw or blanched.

Szechuan Vegetable Lo Mein

2 cans (about 14 ounces each) vegetable or chicken broth

2 teaspoons minced garlic

1 teaspoon minced fresh ginger

¼ teaspoon red pepper flakes

1 package (16 ounces) frozen vegetable medley, such as broccoli, carrots, water chestnuts and red bell peppers

1 package (5 ounces) Asian curly noodles or 5 ounces angel hair pasta, broken in half

3 tablespoons soy sauce

1 tablespoon dark sesame oil

¼ cup thinly sliced green onion tops

1. Combine broth, garlic, ginger and red pepper flakes in large deep skillet. Cover and bring to a boil over high heat.

2. Add vegetables and noodles to skillet; cover and return to a boil. Reduce heat to medium-low; simmer, uncovered, 5 to 6 minutes or until noodles and vegetables are tender, stirring occasionally.

3. Stir soy sauce and sesame oil into broth mixture; cook 3 minutes. Stir in green onions; ladle into bowls.   *Makes 4 servings*

Prep and Cook Time: 20 minutes

Note: For a heartier, protein-packed main dish, add 1 package (10½ ounces) extra-firm tofu, cut into ¾-inch pieces, to the broth mixture with the soy sauce and sesame oil.

Chunky Garden Stew

Spicy Hot Sauce (recipe follows)
1 tablespoon olive or canola oil
3 medium Colorado Sangre red potatoes, cut into chunks
1 large carrot, sliced diagonally
1 medium onion, quartered
1 large yellow squash or zucchini, sliced
1 Japanese eggplant *or* ½ regular eggplant, cut into cubes
2 stalks celery, sliced
1 small red or green bell pepper, cut into chunks
1 teaspoon *each* ground cinnamon, ground coriander and ground turmeric
½ teaspoon *each* salt, ground cumin and ground cardamom
2 cans (14½ ounces each) vegetable broth
1 can (15 ounces) chick-peas, drained
⅔ cup raisins
6 cups hot cooked rice

Prepare Spicy Hot Sauce; set aside. Heat oil in Dutch oven over medium-high heat. Add potatoes and carrot; cook and stir 5 minutes. Add onion, squash, eggplant, celery, bell pepper, spices and salt; cook and stir 3 to 5 minutes. Add broth, chick-peas and raisins; bring to a simmer. Simmer, covered, about 15 minutes or until potatoes are tender. Serve vegetable stew over rice. Serve with Spicy Hot Sauce. *Makes 5 to 6 servings*

Spicy Hot Sauce

⅓ cup coarsely chopped fresh cilantro
¼ cup water
1 tablespoon olive or canola oil
2 cloves garlic
½ teaspoon *each* salt and ground turmeric
¼ to ½ teaspoon ground red pepper
¼ teaspoon *each* sugar, ground cumin, ground cardamom and ground coriander

Combine all ingredients in blender; process until smooth. Adjust flavors to taste. *Makes about ½ cup sauce*

*Favorite recipe from **Colorado Potato Administrative Committee***

Chunky Garden Stew

Spinach-Cheese Pasta Casserole

8 ounces uncooked pasta shells
2 eggs
1 cup ricotta cheese
1 package (10 ounces) frozen chopped spinach, thawed and squeezed dry
1 jar (26 ounces) marinara sauce
1 teaspoon salt
1 cup (4 ounces) shredded mozzarella cheese
¼ cup grated Parmesan cheese

1. Preheat oven to 350°F. Spray 1½-quart round casserole with nonstick cooking spray. Cook pasta according to package directions until al dente; drain.

2. Meanwhile, whisk eggs in bowl until blended. Add ricotta and spinach to eggs; stir until blended. Stir in pasta, marinara sauce and salt until pasta is well coated. Pour into prepared dish; sprinkle evenly with mozzarella and Parmesan.

3. Bake, covered, 30 minutes. Uncover and bake 15 minutes or until hot and bubbly.   *Makes 6 to 8 servings*

Quick Veg•All® Enchiladas

1 can (15 ounces) VEG•ALL® Original Mixed Vegetables, drained
1 can (15 ounces) refried beans
8 (6-inch) corn tortillas
1 can (10 ounces) enchilada sauce
1 cup shredded cheddar cheese
1 cup sour cream
½ cup chopped green onions
½ cup chopped ripe olives

Preheat oven to 350°F. Combine Veg•All and beans in medium bowl. Divide mixture and place in center of each tortilla; roll up. Place rolled tortillas in baking dish. Cover tortillas with enchilada sauce and cheese. Bake for 30 minutes. Top with sour cream, green onions and olives.

Makes 4 servings

Prep Time: 7 minutes
Cook Time: 30 minutes

Note: If tortillas unfold as you are assembling them, turn seam-side down.

Spinach-Cheese Pasta Casserole

Vegetable & Tofu Gratin

Nonstick cooking spray
1 teaspoon olive oil
¾ cup thinly sliced fennel bulb
¾ cup thinly sliced onion
2 cloves garlic, minced
¾ cup cooked brown rice
2 tablespoons balsamic or red wine vinegar, divided
2 teaspoons dried Italian seasoning, divided
3 ounces firm tofu, crumbled
¼ cup crumbled feta cheese
2 to 3 ripe plum tomatoes, sliced ¼ inch thick
1 medium zucchini, sliced ¼ inch thick
⅛ teaspoon salt
⅛ teaspoon black pepper
¼ cup fresh bread crumbs
2 tablespoons freshly grated Parmesan cheese

1. Preheat oven to 400°F. Spray 1-quart shallow baking dish with cooking spray.

2. Spray medium skillet with cooking spray. Heat oil in medium skillet over medium heat until hot. Add fennel and onion. Cook about 10 minutes or until tender and lightly browned, stirring frequently. Add garlic; cook and stir 1 minute. Spread over bottom of prepared baking dish.

3. Combine rice, 1 tablespoon vinegar and ½ teaspoon Italian seasoning in small bowl. Spread over onion mixture.

4. Combine tofu, feta cheese, remaining 1 tablespoon vinegar and 1 teaspoon Italian seasoning in same small bowl; toss to blend. Spoon over rice. Top with alternating rows of tomato and zucchini slices. Sprinkle with salt and pepper.

5. Combine bread crumbs, Parmesan cheese and remaining ½ teaspoon Italian seasoning in small bowl. Sprinkle over top. Spray bread crumb topping lightly with nonstick cooking spray. Bake 30 minutes or until heated through and topping is browned. *Makes 2 servings*

Vegetable & Tofu Gratin

Eggplant Parmigiana

2 eggs, beaten
¼ cup milk
   Dash garlic powder
   Dash onion powder
   Dash salt
   Dash black pepper
1 large eggplant, cut into ½-inch-thick slices
½ cup seasoned dry bread crumbs
   Vegetable oil for frying
1 jar (about 26 ounces) spaghetti sauce
4 cups (16 ounces) shredded mozzarella cheese
2½ cups (10 ounces) shredded Swiss cheese
¼ cup grated Parmesan cheese
¼ cup grated Romano cheese

1. Preheat oven to 350°F. Combine eggs, milk, garlic powder, onion powder, salt and pepper in shallow bowl. Dip eggplant into egg mixture; coat in bread crumbs.

2. Add enough oil to large skillet to cover bottom by ¼ inch. Heat over medium-high heat. Brown eggplant in batches on both sides; drain on paper towels. Cover bottom of 13×9-inch baking dish with 2 to 3 tablespoons spaghetti sauce. Layer half of eggplant, half of mozzarella cheese, half of Swiss cheese and half of remaining sauce in dish. Repeat layers. Sprinkle with Parmesan and Romano cheeses.

3. Bake 30 minutes or until heated through and cheeses are melted.

Makes 4 servings

Eggplant Parmigiana

Slow Cooker

Chicken Stew

4 to 5 cups chopped cooked chicken (about 5 boneless skinless chicken breasts)
1 can (28 ounces) whole tomatoes, cut up, undrained
2 large potatoes, cut into 1-inch pieces
8 ounces fresh okra, sliced
1 large onion, chopped
1 can (14 ounces) cream-style corn
½ cup ketchup
½ cup barbecue sauce

Slow Cooker Directions

1. Combine chicken, tomatoes with juice, potatoes, okra and onion in slow cooker. Cover; cook on LOW 6 to 8 hours or until potatoes are tender.

2. Add corn, ketchup and barbecue sauce. Cover; cook on HIGH 30 minutes.   *Makes 6 servings*

Prep Time: 15 minutes
Cook Time: 6½ to 8½ hours

Chicken Stew

Beef with Apples & Sweet Potatoes

1 boneless beef chuck shoulder roast (2 pounds)
1 can (40 ounces) sweet potatoes, drained
2 small onions, sliced
2 apples, cored and sliced
½ cup beef broth
2 cloves garlic, minced
1 teaspoon salt
1 teaspoon dried thyme, divided
¾ teaspoon black pepper, divided
1 tablespoon cornstarch
¼ teaspoon ground cinnamon
2 tablespoons cold water

Slow Cooker Directions

1. Trim and discard fat from beef. Cut beef into 2-inch pieces. Place beef, sweet potatoes, onions, apples, beef broth, garlic, salt, ½ teaspoon thyme and ½ teaspoon pepper in 4-quart slow cooker. Cover; cook on LOW 8 to 9 hours.

2. Transfer beef, sweet potatoes and apples to platter; keep warm. Let liquid stand 5 minutes to allow fat to rise. Skim off and discard fat.

3. Stir together cornstarch, remaining ½ teaspoon thyme, ¼ teaspoon pepper, cinnamon and water until smooth; stir into cooking liquid. Cook 15 minutes on HIGH or until juices are thickened. Serve sauce with beef, sweet potatoes and apples. *Makes 6 servings*

Prep Time: 20 minutes
Cook Time: 8 to 9 hours

Beef with Apples & Sweet Potatoes

Pork & Tomato Ragoût

2 pounds pork stew meat, cut into 1-inch pieces
¼ cup all-purpose flour
3 tablespoons oil
1¼ cups white wine
2 pounds red potatoes, cut into ½-inch pieces
1 can (about 14 ounces) diced tomatoes
1 cup finely chopped onion
1 cup water
½ cup finely chopped celery
2 cloves garlic, minced
½ teaspoon black pepper
1 stick cinnamon
3 tablespoons chopped fresh parsley

Slow Cooker Directions

1. Toss pork with flour. Heat oil in large skillet over medium-high heat. Add pork to skillet; brown on all sides. Place pork in slow cooker.

2. Add wine to skillet; bring to a boil, scraping up browned bits from bottom of skillet. Pour into slow cooker.

3. Add all remaining ingredients except parsley. Cover; cook on LOW 6 to 8 hours or until pork and potatoes are tender. Remove and discard cinnamon stick. Adjust seasonings, if desired. Sprinkle with parsley just before serving.

Makes 6 servings

Cook Time: 6 to 8 hours

A ragoût is a thick stew made from pieces of meat, poultry or fish that are browned in fat and then cooked slowly with stock and seasonings. Vegetables are often added as well. Typically French, ragoûts are similar to simple stews and braises. The terms are often used interchangeably.

Pork & Tomato Ragoût

Three-Bean Turkey Chili

1 pound ground turkey
1 small onion, chopped
1 can (28 ounces) diced tomatoes, undrained
1 can (15 ounces) chickpeas, rinsed and drained
1 can (15 ounces) kidney beans, rinsed and drained
1 can (15 ounces) black beans, rinsed and drained
1 can (8 ounces) tomato sauce
1 can (4 ounces) diced mild green chiles
1 to 2 tablespoons chili powder

Slow Cooker Directions

1. Cook and stir turkey and onion in medium skillet over medium-high heat until turkey is no longer pink. Drain fat. Place turkey mixture into slow cooker.

2. Add remaining ingredients; mix well. Cover; cook on HIGH 6 to 8 hours.

Makes 6 to 8 servings

Cook Time: 6 to 8 hours

Simple Slow Cooker Pork Roast

4 to 5 red potatoes, cut into bite-size pieces
4 carrots, cut into bite-size pieces
1 marinated pork loin roast (3 to 4 pounds)
½ cup water
1 package (10 ounces) frozen baby peas
   Salt
   Black pepper

Slow Cooker Directions

Place potatoes, carrots and pork roast in slow cooker. (If necessary, cut roast in half to fit in slow cooker.) Add water. Cover; cook on LOW 6 to 8 hours or until vegetables are tender. Add peas during last hour of cooking. Season to taste with salt and pepper.

Makes 6 servings

Cook Time: 6 to 8 hours

Three-Bean Turkey Chili

Broccoli and Beef Pasta

2 cups broccoli florets *or* 1 package (10 ounces) frozen broccoli, thawed
1 onion, thinly sliced
½ teaspoon dried basil
½ teaspoon dried oregano
½ teaspoon dried thyme
1 can (14½ ounces) Italian-style diced tomatoes, undrained
¾ cup beef broth
1 pound lean ground beef
2 cloves garlic, minced
2 cups cooked rotini pasta
¾ cup (3 ounces) shredded Cheddar cheese or grated Parmesan cheese
2 tablespoons tomato paste

Slow Cooker Directions

1. Layer broccoli, onion, basil, oregano, thyme, tomatoes with juice and broth in slow cooker. Cover; cook on LOW 2½ hours.

2. Cook and stir beef and garlic in large nonstick skillet over medium-high heat until brown, stirring to break up meat. Drain fat. Add beef mixture to slow cooker. Cover; cook 2 hours.

3. Stir in pasta, cheese and tomato paste. Cover; cook 30 minutes or until cheese melts and mixture is heated through. Sprinkle with additional shredded cheese, if desired.   *Makes 4 servings*

Prep Time: 15 minutes
Cook Time: about 5 hours

Broccoli and Beef Pasta

Autumn Vegetables and Pork Chops

6 pork chops, ¾ inch thick
1 medium-size acorn squash
¾ cup packed brown sugar
3 tablespoons chopped green onions
2 tablespoons butter, melted
2 tablespoons orange juice
1 teaspoon Worcestershire sauce
1 teaspoon freshly grated orange peel
¼ teaspoon ground cinnamon
⅛ teaspoon ground nutmeg
2 cups frozen green peas

Slow Cooker Directions
Slice acorn squash in half, remove seeds and slice each half into 6 slices, approximately ½ inch thick. Place 6 half slices on bottom of 5-quart slow cooker. Arrange 3 pork chops over squash; repeat layers. Combine remaining ingredients except peas; pour over squash mixture. Cover and cook on LOW 5 to 6 hours or until pork and squash are tender. Remove both from slow cooker; keep warm. Stir in frozen peas. Turn heat setting to HIGH. Cover and cook about 5 minutes or until peas are tender; drain.   *Makes 6 servings*

Favorite recipe from **National Pork Board**

When grating orange peel, grate only the outer orange
layer of the skin, which is very sweet and flavorful. Avoid
grating into the white pith, as it has a bitter taste.

Arroz con Pollo

    6 chicken thighs, skin removed
    1 can (14½ ounces) chicken broth
    1 can (14½ ounces) stewed tomatoes
    1 package (10 ounces) frozen peas
    1 package (8 ounces) Spanish-style yellow rice mix
 1½ cups *French's*® French Fried Onions, divided

Slow Cooker Directions

1. Coat slow cooker with vegetable cooking spray. Combine chicken, broth and tomatoes in slow cooker. Cover and cook on LOW setting for 4 to 5 hours (or on HIGH for 2 to 2½ hours) until chicken is fork-tender.

2. Stir in peas and rice mix. Cover and cook on LOW setting for 2 to 3 hours (or on HIGH for 1 to 1½ hours) until rice is cooked and all liquid is absorbed. Stir in ¾ *cup* French Fried Onions. Spoon soup into serving bowls; top with remaining onions. *Makes 6 servings*

Prep Time: 10 minutes
Cook Time: 8 hours

Note: Cook times vary depending on type of slow cooker used. Check manufacturer's recommendations for cooking chicken and rice.

Saucy Tropical Turkey

3 to 4 turkey thighs, skin removed (about 2½ pounds)
2 tablespoons vegetable oil
1 small onion, halved and sliced
1 can (20 ounces) pineapple chunks, drained
1 red bell pepper, cubed
⅔ cup apricot preserves
3 tablespoons soy sauce
1 teaspoon grated lemon peel
1 teaspoon ground ginger
¼ cup cold water
2 tablespoons cornstarch
Hot cooked rice

Slow Cooker Directions

1. Rinse turkey and pat dry. Heat oil in large skillet; brown turkey on all sides. Place onion in slow cooker. Transfer turkey to slow cooker; top with pineapple and bell pepper.

2. Combine preserves, soy sauce, lemon peel and ginger in small bowl; mix well. Spoon over turkey. Cover; cook on LOW 6 to 7 hours.

3. Remove turkey from slow cooker; keep warm. Blend water and cornstarch until smooth; stir into slow cooker. Cook, uncovered, on HIGH 15 minutes or until sauce is slightly thickened. Adjust seasonings. Return turkey to slow cooker; cook until hot. Serve with rice. *Makes 6 servings*

Prep Time: 15 minutes
Cook Time: 6½ to 7½ hours

Saucy Tropical Turkey

Classic Cabbage Rolls

  6 cups water
12 large cabbage leaves
  1 pound lean ground lamb
½ cup cooked rice
  1 teaspoon salt
¼ teaspoon dried oregano
¼ teaspoon ground nutmeg
¼ teaspoon black pepper
1½ cups tomato sauce

Slow Cooker Directions

1. Bring water to a boil in large saucepan. Turn off heat. Soak cabbage leaves in water 5 minutes; remove, drain and cool leaves.

2. Combine lamb, rice, salt, oregano, nutmeg and pepper in large bowl; mix well. Place 2 tablespoonfuls mixture in center of each cabbage leaf; roll up firmly. Place cabbage rolls in slow cooker, seam side down. Pour tomato sauce over cabbage rolls.

3. Cover; cook on LOW 8 to 10 hours.   *Makes 6 servings*

Prep Time: 20 minutes
Cook Time: 8 to 10 hours

Classic Cabbage Rolls

Tuscan Pasta

1 pound boneless skinless chicken breasts, cut into 1-inch pieces
2 cans (14½ ounces each) Italian-style stewed tomatoes, undrained
1 can (15 ounces) red kidney beans, rinsed and drained
1 can (15 ounces) tomato sauce
1 cup water
1 jar (4½ ounces) sliced mushrooms, drained
1 medium green bell pepper, chopped
½ cup chopped onion
½ cup chopped celery
4 cloves garlic, minced
1 teaspoon dried Italian seasoning
6 ounces uncooked thin spaghetti, broken in half

Slow Cooker Directions

1. Place all ingredients except spaghetti in slow cooker.

2. Cover; cook on LOW 4 hours or until vegetables are tender.

3. Stir in spaghetti. Cook on HIGH 10 minutes; stir. Cover; cook 35 minutes or until pasta is tender. *Makes 8 servings*

Harvest Ham Supper

6 carrots, cut into 2-inch pieces
3 medium sweet potatoes, quartered
1 to 1½ pounds boneless ham
1 cup maple syrup

Slow Cooker Directions

1. Place carrots and potatoes in bottom of slow cooker. Place ham on top of vegetables. Pour syrup over ham and vegetables.

2. Cover; cook on LOW 6 to 8 hours. *Makes 6 servings*

Prep Time: 10 minutes
Cook Time: 6 to 8 hours

Tuscan Pasta

Cantonese Pork

2 pork tenderloins (about 2 pounds)
1 tablespoon vegetable oil
1 can (8 ounces) pineapple chunks in juice, undrained
1 can (8 ounces) tomato sauce
2 cans (4 ounces each) sliced mushrooms, drained
1 medium onion, thinly sliced
3 tablespoons brown sugar
2 tablespoons Worcestershire sauce
1½ teaspoons salt
1½ teaspoons white vinegar
    Hot cooked rice

Slow Cooker Directions

1. Cut tenderloins in half lengthwise, then crosswise into ¼-inch-thick slices. Heat oil in large nonstick skillet over medium-low heat. Brown pork on all sides. Drain and discard fat.

2. Place pork, pineapple with juice, tomato sauce, mushrooms, onion, brown sugar, Worcestershire, salt and vinegar in slow cooker.

3. Cover; cook on LOW 6 to 8 hours or on HIGH 4 hours. Serve over rice.

Makes 8 servings

Prep Time: 15 minutes
Cook Time: 6 to 8 hours

Worcestershire sauce is a dark, savory sauce developed in India and named after the English town, Worcester, where it was first bottled. Made from a complex and seemingly incompatible mix of ingredients, including anchovies, tamarind paste, molasses, onions, garlic and soy sauce, it is used as a seasoning in sauces, gravies and soups.

Cantonese Pork

Layered Mexican-Style Casserole

2 cans (15½ ounces each) hominy,* drained
1 can (15 ounces) black beans, rinsed and drained
1 can (14½ ounces) diced tomatoes with garlic, basil and oregano, undrained
1 cup thick and chunky salsa
1 can (6 ounces) tomato paste
½ teaspoon ground cumin
3 (9-inch) flour tortillas
2 cups (8 ounces) shredded Monterey Jack cheese
¼ cup sliced black olives

Hominy is corn that has been treated to remove the germ and hull. It can be found with the canned vegetables or beans in most supermarkets.

Slow Cooker Directions

1. Prepare foil handles (see below). Spray slow cooker with nonstick cooking spray.

2. Combine hominy, beans, tomatoes with juice, salsa, tomato paste and cumin in large bowl.

3. Press one tortilla in bottom of slow cooker. (Edges of tortilla may turn up slightly.) Top with one third of hominy mixture and one third of cheese. Repeat layers. Press remaining tortilla on top. Top with remaining hominy mixture. Set aside remaining cheese.

4. Cover; cook on LOW 6 to 8 hours. Sprinkle with remaining cheese and olives. Cover; let stand 5 minutes. Pull out tortilla stack with foil handles.

Makes 6 servings

Prep Time: 15 minutes
Cook Time: 6 to 8 hours

Foil Handles: Tear off three 18×2-inch strips of heavy-duty foil or use regular foil folded to double thickness. Crisscross foil strips in spoke design and place into slow cooker to make lifting of tortilla stack easier.

Layered Mexican-Style Casserole

Mediterranean Stew

1 medium butternut or acorn squash, peeled and cut into 1-inch cubes
2 cups unpeeled eggplant, cut into 1-inch cubes
2 cups sliced zucchini
1 can (about 15 ounces) chickpeas, rinsed and drained
1 package (10 ounces) frozen cut okra
1 can (8 ounces) tomato sauce
1 cup chopped onion
1 medium tomato, chopped
1 medium carrot, thinly sliced
½ cup reduced-sodium vegetable broth
⅓ cup raisins
1 clove garlic, minced
½ teaspoon ground cumin
½ teaspoon ground turmeric
¼ to ½ teaspoon ground red pepper
¼ teaspoon ground cinnamon
¼ teaspoon paprika
6 to 8 cups hot cooked couscous or rice
    Fresh parsley (optional)

Slow Cooker Directions

1. Combine squash, eggplant, zucchini, chickpeas, okra, tomato sauce, onion, tomato, carrot, broth, raisins, garlic, cumin, turmeric, red pepper, cinnamon and paprika in slow cooker; mix well. Cover; cook on LOW 8 to 10 hours or until vegetables are crisp-tender.

2. Serve mixture over couscous. Garnish with parsley.   *Makes 6 servings*

Cook Time: 8 to 10 hours

Mediterranean Stew

Chicken Pilaf

2 pounds chopped cooked chicken
2 cans (8 ounces each) tomato sauce
2½ cups water
1⅓ cups uncooked long-grain converted rice
1 cup chopped onion
1 cup chopped celery
1 cup chopped green bell pepper
⅔ cup sliced black olives
¼ cup sliced almonds
¼ cup (½ stick) butter
2 cloves garlic, minced
2½ teaspoons salt
½ teaspoon ground allspice
½ teaspoon ground turmeric
¼ teaspoon curry powder
¼ teaspoon black pepper

Slow Cooker Directions

1. Combine all ingredients in slow cooker; stir well.

2. Cover; cook on LOW 6 to 8 hours or on HIGH 3 to 4 hours.

Makes 10 servings

Prep Time: 15 minutes
Cook Time: 6 to 8 hours

Chicken Pilaf

Barbara's Pork Chop Dinner

1 tablespoon butter
1 tablespoon olive oil
6 pork loin chops
1 can (10¾ ounces) condensed cream of chicken soup, undiluted
1 can (4 ounces) sliced mushrooms, drained and chopped
¼ cup Dijon mustard
¼ cup chicken broth
2 cloves garlic, minced
½ teaspoon salt
½ teaspoon dried basil
¼ teaspoon black pepper
6 red potatoes, unpeeled, cut into thin slices
1 onion, sliced
   Chopped fresh parsley

Slow Cooker Directions

1. Heat butter and oil in large skillet. Brown pork chops on both sides; set aside.

2. Combine soup, mushrooms, mustard, chicken broth, garlic, salt, basil and pepper in slow cooker. Add potatoes and onion; stir to coat. Place pork chops on top of potato mixture.

3. Cover; cook on LOW 8 to 10 hours or on HIGH 4 to 5 hours. Sprinkle with parsley just before serving. *Makes 6 servings*

Prep Time: 15 minutes
Cook Time: 8 to 10 hours

Barbara's Pork Chop Dinner

Shelby Slow Cooker Rouladen

12 pieces top round beef, pounded thin (¼ inch thick)
   Salt and black pepper
   Garlic pepper
 4 tablespoons Dijon mustard
1½ cups chopped onions
1½ cups chopped dill pickles
   Nonstick cooking spray
 ¼ cup (½ stick) butter
 5 tablespoons all-purpose flour
 2 cans (14½ ounces each) beef broth
16 ounces baby carrots
 4 stalks celery, cut into 1-inch pieces

Slow Cooker Directions

1. Season beef with salt, black pepper and garlic pepper. Spread each piece with 1 teaspoon mustard; top with 2 tablespoons each onion and pickles. Starting at one short side of each beef piece fold long edges over, then roll beef tightly. Secure with toothpick.

2. Spray large nonstick skillet with cooking spray. Brown beef rolls in batches in large skillet over medium-high heat. Remove from skillet.

3. In same skillet, melt butter. Add flour. Cook and stir 1 minute. Add beef broth, stirring constantly. Cook and stir until mixture thickens.

4. Pour half of broth mixture into slow cooker. Add carrots and celery; top with beef rolls; pour remaining broth mixture into slow cooker.

5. Cover; cook on LOW 8 to 10 hours or on HIGH 4 to 5 hours until beef is tender. *Makes 6 to 8 servings*

Cook Time: 8 to 10 hours

Turkey Breast with Barley-Cranberry Stuffing

    2 cups reduced-sodium chicken broth
    1 cup uncooked quick-cooking barley
    ½ cup chopped onion
    ½ cup dried cranberries
    2 tablespoons slivered almonds, toasted
    ½ teaspoon rubbed sage
    ½ teaspoon garlic-pepper seasoning
      Nonstick cooking spray
    1 fresh or thawed frozen bone-in turkey breast half (about 2 pounds), skinned
    ⅓ cup finely chopped fresh parsley

Slow Cooker Directions

1. Combine broth, barley, onion, cranberries, almonds, sage and garlic-pepper seasoning in slow cooker.

2. Spray large nonstick skillet with cooking spray. Heat over medium heat until hot. Brown turkey breast on all sides; add to slow cooker. Cover; cook on LOW 4 to 6 hours.

3. Transfer turkey to cutting board; cover with foil and let stand 10 to 15 minutes before carving. Stir parsley into sauce mixture in slow cooker. Serve sliced turkey with sauce and stuffing. *Makes 6 servings*

Prep Time: 10 minutes
Cook Time: 4 to 6 hours
Stand Time: 10 to 15 minutes

Mexicali Chicken

2 medium green bell peppers, cut into thin strips
1 large onion, quartered and thinly sliced
4 chicken thighs, skin removed
4 chicken drumsticks, skin removed
1 tablespoon chili powder
2 teaspoons dried oregano
1 jar (16 ounces) chipotle salsa
½ cup ketchup
2 teaspoons ground cumin
½ teaspoon salt
    Hot cooked noodles

Slow Cooker Directions

1. Place bell peppers and onion in slow cooker; top with chicken. Sprinkle chili powder and oregano evenly over chicken. Add salsa. Cover; cook on LOW 7 to 8 hours or on HIGH 3 to 4 hours.

2. Remove chicken pieces to serving bowl; keep warm. Stir ketchup, cumin and salt into liquid in slow cooker. Cook, uncovered, on HIGH 15 minutes or until hot.

3. Pour mixture over chicken. Serve with noodles.   *Makes 4 servings*

Prep Time: 10 minutes
Cook Time: 7 to 8 hours

Tip: For thicker sauce, blend 1 tablespoon cornstarch and 2 tablespoons water until smooth. Stir into cooking liquid with ketchup, cumin and salt.

Mexicali Chicken

Beef Stew with Molasses and Raisins

⅓ cup all-purpose flour
2 teaspoons salt, divided
1½ teaspoons black pepper, divided
2 pounds boneless beef chuck roast, cut into 1½-inch pieces
5 tablespoons oil, divided
2 medium onions, sliced
1 can (28 ounces) diced tomatoes, drained
1 cup beef broth
3 tablespoons molasses
2 tablespoons cider vinegar
4 cloves garlic, minced
2 teaspoons dried thyme
1 teaspoon celery salt
1 bay leaf
1 small package (8 ounces) baby carrots, cut into halves lengthwise
2 parsnips, diced
½ cup golden raisins

Slow Cooker Directions

1. Combine flour, 1½ teaspoons salt and 1 teaspoon pepper in large bowl. Toss beef in flour mixture. Heat 2 tablespoons oil in large skillet or Dutch oven over medium-high heat. Add half of beef; brown on all sides. Remove browned beef; set aside. Repeat with 2 tablespoons oil and remaining beef.

2. Add remaining 1 tablespoon oil to skillet. Add onions; cook and stir about 5 minutes, scraping up any browned bits from bottom of skillet. Add tomatoes, broth, molasses, vinegar, garlic, thyme, celery salt, bay leaf and remaining ½ teaspoon salt and ½ teaspoon pepper. Bring to a boil. Add browned beef; boil 1 minute.

3. Transfer mixture to slow cooker. Cover; cook on LOW 5 hours or on HIGH 2½ hours. Add carrots, parsnips and raisins. Cook 1 to 2 hours more or until vegetables are tender. Remove and discard bay leaf. *Makes 6 to 8 servings*

Beef Stew with Molasses and Raisins

Turkey Mushroom Stew

1 pound turkey cutlets, cut into 4×1-inch strips
1 small onion, thinly sliced
8 ounces mushrooms, sliced
2 tablespoons minced green onion
1 cup half-and-half or milk
2 to 3 tablespoons all-purpose flour
1 teaspoon salt
1 teaspoon dried tarragon
    Black pepper
½ cup frozen peas
½ cup sour cream
    Puff pastry shells

Slow Cooker Directions

1. Layer turkey, onion, mushrooms and green onion in slow cooker. Cover; cook on LOW 4 hours.

2. Remove turkey and vegetables to serving bowl. Combine half-and-half, flour, salt, tarragon and pepper until smooth. Stir into slow cooker. Return turkey and cooked vegetables to slow cooker. Stir in peas. Cover; cook on HIGH 30 to 45 minutes or until sauce has thickened and peas are heated through.

3. Stir in sour cream just before serving. Serve in puff pastry shells.

Makes 4 servings

To clean fresh mushrooms, wipe them with a damp paper towel, brush with a mushroom brush or soft toothbrush, or rinse briefly under cold running water to remove the dirt. Pat them dry before using. Never soak mushrooms in water because they will absorb it and become mushy.

Turkey Mushroom Stew

Yankee Pot Roast and Vegetables

1 beef chuck pot roast (2½ pounds)
   Salt and black pepper
3 unpeeled medium baking potatoes (about 1 pound), cut into quarters
2 large carrots, cut into ¾-inch slices
2 stalks celery, cut into ¾-inch slices
1 medium onion, sliced
1 large parsnip, cut into ¾-inch slices
2 bay leaves
1 teaspoon dried rosemary
½ teaspoon dried thyme
½ cup reduced-sodium beef broth

Slow Cooker Directions

1. Trim and discard excess fat from meat. Cut meat into serving-size pieces; sprinkle with salt and pepper.

2. Combine vegetables, bay leaves, rosemary and thyme in slow cooker. Place beef over vegetables. Pour broth over beef. Cover; cook on LOW 8½ to 9 hours or until beef is fork-tender.

3. Transfer beef to serving platter. Arrange vegetables around beef. Remove and discard bay leaves. *Makes 10 to 12 servings*

Prep Time: 10 minutes
Cook Time: 8½ to 9 hours

Note: To make gravy, ladle the juices into a 2-cup measure; let stand 5 minutes. Skim off and discard fat. Measure remaining juices and heat to a boil in small saucepan. For each cup of juice, mix 2 tablespoons of flour with ¼ cup of cold water until smooth. Stir mixture into boiling juices, stirring constantly 1 minute or until thickened.

Yankee Pot Roast and Vegetables

Easy Slow-Cooked Chili

2 pounds lean ground beef
2 tablespoons chili powder
1 tablespoon ground cumin
1 can (28 ounces) crushed tomatoes in purée, undrained
1 can (15 ounces) red kidney beans, drained and rinsed
1 cup water
2 cups *French's*® French Fried Onions,* divided
¼ cup *Frank's*® *RedHot*® Original Cayenne Pepper Sauce
   Sour cream and shredded Cheddar cheese

*For added Cheddar flavor, substitute **French's**® **Cheddar French Fried Onions** for the original flavor.*

Slow Cooker Directions

1. Cook ground beef, chili powder and cumin in large nonstick skillet over medium heat until browned, stirring frequently; drain. Transfer to slow cooker.

2. Stir in tomatoes with juice, beans, water, *½ cup* French Fried Onions and *Frank's RedHot* Sauce.

3. Cover; cook on LOW setting for 6 hours (or on HIGH for 3 hours). Serve chili topped with sour cream, cheese and remaining onions.

Makes 8 servings

Prep Time: 10 minutes
Cook Time: 6 hours

Cumin is used extensively in Mexican, Middle Eastern, North African and Indian cooking. Use it sparingly (or add a little at a time), as it is a potent spice and will dominate most other flavors in a dish.

Easy Slow-Cooked Chili

Deviled Beef Short Rib Stew

4 pounds beef short ribs, trimmed
2 pounds small red potatoes, scrubbed and scored
8 carrots, peeled and cut into chunks
2 onions, cut into thick wedges
1 bottle (12 ounces) beer or non-alcoholic malt beverage
8 tablespoons *French's*® Spicy Brown Mustard, divided
3 tablespoons *French's*® Worcestershire Sauce, divided
2 tablespoons cornstarch

Slow Cooker Directions

1. Broil ribs 6 inches from heat on rack in broiler pan 10 minutes or until well browned, turning once. Place vegetables in bottom of slow cooker. Place ribs on top of vegetables.

2. Combine beer, *6 tablespoons* mustard and *2 tablespoons* Worcestershire in medium bowl. Pour into slow cooker. Cover and cook on HIGH setting for 5 hours* or until meat is tender.

3. Transfer meat and vegetables to platter; keep warm. Strain fat from broth; pour broth into saucepan. Combine cornstarch with *2 tablespoons cold water* in small bowl. Stir into broth with remaining *2 tablespoons* mustard and *1 tablespoon* Worcestershire. Heat to boiling. Reduce heat to medium-low. Cook 1 to 2 minutes or until thickened, stirring often. Pass gravy with meat and vegetables. Serve meat with additional mustard.

Makes 6 servings (with 3 cups gravy)

*Or cook 10 hours on LOW setting.

Hint: Prepare ingredients the night before for quick assembly in the morning. Keep refrigerated until ready to use.

Tip: Use a barley wine or spiced winter ale in this stew for an even bolder beef flavor.

Deviled Beef Short Rib Stew

Pork Meatballs & Sauerkraut

1¼ **pounds lean ground pork**
¾ **cup dry bread crumbs**
1 **egg, lightly beaten**
2 **tablespoons milk**
2 **teaspoons caraway seeds, divided**
1 **teaspoon salt**
½ **teaspoon Worcestershire sauce**
¼ **teaspoon black pepper**
1 **jar (32 ounces) sauerkraut, drained, squeezed dry and snipped**
½ **cup chopped onion**
6 **slices bacon, crisp-cooked and crumbled**
   Chopped fresh parsley

Slow Cooker Directions

1. Combine ground pork, bread crumbs, egg, milk, 1 teaspoon caraway seeds, salt, Worcestershire and pepper in large bowl. Shape mixture into 2-inch balls. Brown meatballs in large nonstick skillet over medium-high heat.

2. Combine sauerkraut, onion, bacon and remaining 1 teaspoon caraway seeds in slow cooker. Place meatballs on top of sauerkraut mixture.

3. Cover; cook on LOW 6 to 8 hours. Sprinkle with chopped parsley.

Makes 4 to 6 servings

Prep Time: 30 minutes
Cook Time: 6 to 8 hours

❧ *Acknowledgments* ❧

The publisher would like to thank the companies and organizations listed below for the use of their recipes and photographs in this publication.

Bays English Muffin Corporation

Birds Eye Foods

Bob Evans®

California Poultry Federation

Colorado Potato Administrative Committee

Del Monte Corporation

Filippo Berio® Olive Oil

Florida Department of Agriculture and Consumer Services, Bureau of Seafood and Aquaculture

Florida's Citrus Growers

The Golden Grain Company®

Grandma's® is a registered trademark of Mott's, LLP

The Hidden Valley® Food Products Company

Hillshire Farm®

Hormel Foods, LLC

Jennie-O Turkey Store®

MASTERFOODS USA

McIlhenny Company (TABASCO® brand Pepper Sauce)

Minnesota Cultivated Wild Rice Council

National Fisheries Institute

National Honey Board

National Pork Board

National Turkey Federation

Nestlé USA

Newman's Own, Inc.®

Norseland, Inc.
Lucini Italia Co.

North Dakota Beef Commission

North Dakota Wheat Commission

Reckitt Benckiser Inc.

Riviana Foods Inc.

Sargento® Foods Inc.

Sauder's Quality Eggs

StarKist Seafood Company

Stonyfield Farm®

Unilever

USA Rice Federation

Veg•All®

Wisconsin Milk Marketing Board

Index

VOLUME MEASUREMENTS (dry)

1/8 teaspoon = 0.5 mL
1/4 teaspoon = 1 mL
1/2 teaspoon = 2 mL
3/4 teaspoon = 4 mL
1 teaspoon = 5 mL
1 tablespoon = 15 mL
2 tablespoons = 30 mL
1/4 cup = 60 mL
1/3 cup = 75 mL
1/2 cup = 125 mL
2/3 cup = 150 mL
3/4 cup = 175 mL
1 cup = 250 mL
2 cups = 1 pint = 500 mL
3 cups = 750 mL
4 cups = 1 quart = 1 L

VOLUME MEASUREMENTS (fluid)

1 fluid ounce (2 tablespoons) = 30 mL
4 fluid ounces (1/2 cup) = 125 mL
8 fluid ounces (1 cup) = 250 mL
12 fluid ounces (1 1/2 cups) = 375 mL
16 fluid ounces (2 cups) = 500 mL

WEIGHTS (mass)

1/2 ounce = 15 g
1 ounce = 30 g
3 ounces = 90 g
4 ounces = 120 g
8 ounces = 225 g
10 ounces = 285 g
12 ounces = 360 g
16 ounces = 1 pound = 450 g

DIMENSIONS

1/16 inch = 2 mm
1/8 inch = 3 mm
1/4 inch = 6 mm
1/2 inch = 1.5 cm
3/4 inch = 2 cm
1 inch = 2.5 cm

OVEN TEMPERATURES

250°F = 120°C
275°F = 140°C
300°F = 150°C
325°F = 160°C
350°F = 180°C
375°F = 190°C
400°F = 200°C
425°F = 220°C
450°F = 230°C

BAKING PAN SIZES

Utensil	Size in Inches/Quarts	Metric Volume	Size in Centimeters
Baking or Cake Pan (square or rectangular)	8×8×2	2 L	20×20×5
	9×9×2	2.5 L	23×23×5
	12×8×2	3 L	30×20×5
	13×9×2	3.5 L	33×23×5
Loaf Pan	8×4×3	1.5 L	20×10×7
	9×5×3	2 L	23×13×7
Round Layer Cake Pan	8×1½	1.2 L	20×4
	9×1½	1.5 L	23×4
Pie Plate	8×1¼	750 mL	20×3
	9×1¼	1 L	23×3
Baking Dish or Casserole	1 quart	1 L	—
	1½ quart	1.5 L	—
	2 quart	2 L	—